BE A FATHER TO YOUR CHILD

BAF

[REAL TALK
FROM BLACK MEN ON
FAMILY, LOVE,
AND FATHERHOOD]

EDITED BY APRIL R. SILVER

Library of Congress Cataloging-in-Publication Data

Be a father to your child : family, love, and manhood as told from the hearts of
black men / edited by April R. Silver.
    p. cm.
 Includes bibliographical references.
 ISBN-13: 978-1-59376-192-9
 ISBN-10: 1-59376-192-9
 1. African American fathers. 2. African American men—Family relationships.
3. Fatherhood—United States. I. Silver, April R.

HQ756.B388 2008
306.874'208996073—dc22

                        2007050487

Book Design by Timothy Goodman

Printed in the United States of America

Soft Skull Press
An Imprint of Counterpoint LLC
2117 Fourth Street
Suite D
Berkeley CA 94710

www.softskull.com
www.counterpointpress.com

Distributed by Publishers Group West

10 9 8 7 6 5 4 3 2 1

Contents

SIDE B

A Dedication and Opening Meditation

▸ There is an ancient African proverb that teaches "We come here so that we may learn how to be better ancestors." To our collective enlightened ancestors who kneel before God, including those who were enslaved Africans, we acknowledge your sacrifice and give thanks for your everlasting wisdom. We seek a clear head, a clean heart, clean hands, and a clear path so that we may pass on the richest blessings.

▸ [Mr. Eddie Silver, Jr.]

Shout Outs

▶ Colleagues told me that editing an anthology is indeed *work*: many moving parts. I believed them, but there's nothing like your own *knowing*. But as one of my mentors says, "at the end of the day and in the morning," many blessings can be found during the journey. I am truly humbled and grateful to be a part of this project. When it was enjoyable, it was because I was inspired by the honesty and courage of the men who volunteered to tell their stories. For many of them, this project was confronting and intrusive. It kicked up a lot of old feelings, previous and lingering pains, and some unresolved emotional baggage, but they waded through it all. So a BIG SHOUT OUT goes to Aaron Lloyd, Adisa Banjoko, Al Young, Bakari Kitwana, Bill Stephney, Byron Hurt, Cheo Tyehimba, Davey D., Dion Chavis, James Peterson, Jelani Cobb, Kevin Powell, Kevin Williams, Lasana Hotep, Loren Harris, Lumumba Akinwole-Bandele, Mo Beasley, Rhymefest, Saddi Khali, Shaun Neblett, Steven Fullwood, Talib Kweli, Thabiti Boone, and Tim Jones. I am honored to know you all and feel blessed that you trusted me to escort your stories to the world through these pages.

A special shout out to Loren Harris of The Ford Foundation for his BOLD vision in pushing for this work. For many years now, your intelligence, compassion, and wisdom have elevated me. Thank you also to the Twenty-first Century Foundation and the *Black Men and Boys Initiative* for being steady on the case and for standing up for Black males. A big shout out also to Richard Nash and Anne Horowitz of Soft Skull Press for your faith and patience. For their hard work, tips of the trade, guidance, insights, critiques, or kind words of encouragement, I especially thank Jenny B. Silver and Eddie Omar Silver; Craig Brown; Akanke Washington; Kevin Powell; Marie Brown of Marie Brown and Associates; Retha Powers; Dr. Brenda Greene, Dr. Perry Greene, and Midori Nishijima; Maeshay K. Lewis, Drake Holliday, Thysha Shabazz, Zed Lloyd, John Knight Smith, and the entire team at AKILA WORKSONGS, Inc.

Nationwide, there are countless fathers and fatherhood activists whose daily grind is "fairness for fathers." They seek justice through a variety of venues and outlets: They represent positive fatherhood models in the family courtrooms, in the parks with their children, parenting centers, the media, policy boardrooms, fatherhood conferences, or in the intimacy of their own homes. Many fathers and father–like figures often find themselves, in the quiet of the night, contemplating the madness of the system—coiled in fetal positions, trying to figure out how to be the best father they can be. To those people (known and unknown), we honor you with this effort. The world will indeed be a better place if you stay steady and seek higher ground.

And because we are contemplating hip hop and fatherhood at its core level, we owe a million thank-yous to Kool Herc (the Father of Hip Hop), Afrika Bambaataa (the Godfather of Hip Hop), and all the other founding fathers and early trailblazers. You all have birthed more sons and daughters than the world or your offspring give you credit for. Given the current state of hip hop, it seems that most of your children have abandoned *the teachings*, but not all of the people are lost all of the time. You represent what is right about hip hop so we go to work . . . inspired. Like you, we hope to add more light than darkness to the world.

A special shout out to Ed O.G. and Da Bulldogs. The title of this book is named after their 1991 hit "Be a Father to Your Child." Sadly, nearly twenty years later, the relevance is still not lost. That simple yet enduring call to action inspired a generation of young men. Thank you for having the courage to tell the truth. It matters that in hip hop we have a soundtrack for the truth.

Lastly, this daddy's girl has an *extra* special shout out to my *dae-dee*, Eddie Silver, Jr.—my loving father and my first guidepost to the culture and music of Black people. Thank you for being a wonderful human being. Your firstborn seeks to keep you smiling.

Introduction

▸   I began producing events on the issue of Black fatherhood in 1999. My focus has always been Black fathers of the hip hop generation. My team of consultants and I, with the support of the Mott Foundation and the National Center for Strategic Nonprofit Planning and Community Leadership (NPCL), produced "A Father's Story: Hip Hop Dads Speak Out!" in April of that year. The following year, we produced a town hall meeting at Abyssinian Baptist Church in Harlem. Same topic, different players. In all, we connected with Malik Yoba, Mos Def, Bill Stephney, and a number of other father-artist-advocates whose names and reputations were known. The whole point was to draw people's attention to the obvious: Black families, in general, are suffering and a critical part of any solution must deal with young Black men and young Black fathers.

  Particularly since the 1990s, there has emerged a powerful wave of interest in the "issue" of young Black fathers. Policy makers, scholars, lawmakers, grant-makers, and other resource circles have contemplated some harsh realities: today, 70 percent of African

American children are born to parents who are not married (a huge spike from the mid-1960s); about 60 percent of Black children are growing up without their fathers; and joblessness among young Black men is reaching record high numbers. While the economy flourished for Americans overall, Black people caught a bad one. My generation, the so-called Generation X population (roughly defined as those born between 1965 and 1989) was the first of Black children born into households and communities with inordinately high rates of joblessness; fatherlessness; incarceration; illegal drug sale, use, and abuse; and HIV/AIDS prevalence: hardly model environments for family building. Our parents' generation, the so-called Baby Boomers (those born between 1946 and 1964) mostly saw us as selfish, heartless crack babies, with the men being nothing more than gun-toting drug dealers and thugs. We were devoid of culture and morals and if we made it past our teenage years at all, we were likely to be poor, uneducated, and nonproductive—a human garbage pile. Some even labeled us an "endangered species." But we know better. We understand that oppression is a dark reality that defines our historical and current conditions, but it is not our destiny. So in the midst of it all, we persevere.

Stats aside, I am not one that respects the rallying of generational pain, as in "This generation is worse off than that generation," or "We've never seen it this bad for Black people." While pain and suffering have been levied in different ways throughout generations of Black families, our focus should be how to eradicate oppression, not comparing it. In all that we do, however, every generation should endeavor to pour light on the victories seized during our lifetime. That understood, this passion-filled anthology seeks to shed some light on what is good and enduring about a sampling of Black fathers and sons who are committed to creating healthy families. While issues of abuse, abandonment, and absenteeism are common in these collected works, it is simultaneously true that compassion, forgiveness, loyalty, and perseverance are heavily threaded here too.

Unfortunately, this collection has its flaws. It must be acknowledged that, despite this editor's work to engage several gay Black men for this project, this anthology does not have enough voices from our brothers from that community. While there is much more to tell about all the father-son dynamics in the Black community, here is a starting point for consideration.

So in the spirit of striking a positive chord in favor of those Black men who—despite the odds—have not given up on their families, their children, and/or their fathers, and those who have not given up on what's right and beautiful about the world, let this anthology serve as a relevant, empowering perspective . . . real talk, directly from the hearts of a few hip hop heads.

APRIL R. SILVER
Brooklyn
December 2007

[THE SETUP]

To Be Men First, Then Fathers: Realizing Progressive Black Masculinities: An Introduction

▸ LOREN S. HARRIS

In addition to racial oppression, a most troubling issue facing Hip-hop generation Black males is the very limited and often harmful way in which we understand and convey what it means to be masculine; indeed, what it is to be a man. To a large extent the challenge to Black manhood, and womanhood for that matter, is that Black people have had relatively little time throughout our history in America to weigh in any serious sense what gender roles mean. Our generation faces the additional limitation of lacking diverse and healthy models of masculinity. This reality is reflected across the lived experiences of Black people, including Hip-hop culture. As has been true of Hip-hop since the

1970s, this culture and art form born of American poverty and misery reflects the good, bad, and ugly of the larger society.

For example, father absence is a reality in larger American society and is mirrored in Black communities and Hip-hop culture. The majority of Black children are born to unmarried parents who typically part ways before their children reach adulthood. No doubt many of these relationships face challenges from the start. Having little or no money, no place to call home, nor a job, can place unbearable stress on young parents and make building a healthy family unit together nearly impossible. Certainly, stories abound of Hip-hop artists like Jay-Z, Biggie, Eminem, and Tupac (see Kevin Powell's *What Is a Man?* in this anthology) who grew up in households led by a single mother. In many instances, Black men have bailed too soon to really know whether and how they can contribute to the well-being of their child(ren).

Hip-hop culture, like larger American society, can, at best, be described as ambivalent on the issue of fatherlessness. It is as if people who grew up with Hip-hop also grew up with father absence and accepted both as commonplace. For every "Be a Father to Your Child" track (Ed O.G. & Da Bulldogs, 1991) encouraging men to be responsible fathers, there are at least three "Gold Digger" tracks (Kanye West, 2005) reminding men of the downsides of parenting responsibilities. As any responsible parent can bear witness, the commitment is far longer than eighteen years, and that really is the point. Men, particularly Black men, must step up as fathers, yes, but first as responsible men. This process of maturation starts with taking responsibility for our individual sexual behavior by electing to abstain or use a condom, ideally along with some type of female contraceptive to prevent both pregnancy and STDs.

Though it is difficult, we must escape narrow, traditional concepts of manhood and learn to imagine broader and healthier ideas of Black manhood that create openness for diverse expressions of masculinity. Otherwise, we remain prisoners of a societal culture that actively maintains men's dominance over women, gay men, and other vulnerable populations. Successful movements to demand greater human and civil rights have afforded Black people the ability to break away from the ideas of manhood and womanhood that were cultivated by racial injustice. On the real, it is only in the last forty years that Black men and women could seriously take steps to define what it means to be men and women on their own terms.

After more than four hundred years of struggle for racial justice in America, forty years of legal self-determination is hardly a blip on the screen and it is certainly not enough time to deconstruct and redefine *for ourselves* what are appropriate ways for men and women to behave in our communities.

Of course fatherhood is important. A growing body of research is confirming that engaged, supportive, and loving fathers, even those who don't live in the same household, positively impact the lives of their children. However, understood in appropriate historical perspective, the emphasis being placed on Black fatherhood needs to be balanced with attention to the fundamental issues surrounding Black masculinities. As used here, the term masculinities refers to the many definitions and diverse behaviors and ideals for being a man. Use of the term "masculinities" is also meant to suggest there is more than one way to be masculine or manly.

To be sure, the Black community's traditional concerns of poor academic performance, joblessness, incarceration, and father absence among Black men all have roots in racial oppression; but they are also aggravated by us. Too many Black men refuse to relinquish the false pride and comfort found in trying to be like Mike—(pick one) Tiger, Fifty, LeBron, TI—or whoever is the current iconic Black man who American corporate and media interests have propped up before the world as "acceptable." The process of endowing Black men with access to the trappings of mainstream American life that is based on marketability of physical and/or lyrical skills rather than, say, intellectual prowess, is replicated in commercial Hip-hop as well. The commercially successful Black male emcee is financially rewarded for not only his talent but also his portrayal of a character or image approved for global distribution by people outside his community.

These tightly crafted roles of Black manhood are shown around the world and perpetuate the impression that all Black men live within these limits. In turn, many Black men attempt to model the corporate and media-created images put before us. When a Black man is identified as a model of masculinity (approved by corporate endorsers), rest assured he is acceptable to the mainstream America. Take Kobe Bryant or Tiger Woods, for example. They are global sports figures widely applauded by American society as "stand-up guys" and great "pitchmen." (Well, that was true before Kobe caught that rape case.) In this way, Black men are again made commodities, goods or products to be marketed, distributed, and consumed. But since we know full well that not all Black men can (or desire to) achieve global product status, we should reenvision the kinds of Black masculinities that are deemed suitable alternatives to this commercial version of Black manhood.

There is a gripping fear experienced daily by many Black men who comply with stereotypes of Black maleness rather than being themselves. Some of us have been pretending to be that stereotypical Black man for so long we have forgotten who we are and

what our unique contribution to the world is. No doubt some of us are genuinely committed to representing Black culture, but we become complicit in watering down cultural representation when all it means to us is getting up on the latest fad. For example, all over the country Black men can be found with locked hair, a trend that has exploded in the last five to ten years. Hairlocking has cultural significance for many of us and that is a good thing, but for others it is simply an indication of a lack of originality and unwillingness to be caught outside your crew's sanctioned look, whatever that might be. Some of us made a beeline to the tattoo parlor to avoid being the cat without ink on his arm, neck, or face; for others it's having a fresh pair of Air Force Ones or gold—nah, platinum—fronts.

This fear-driven behavior can also be found in our interpersonal relationships, our attitudes about education, and our behavior at the workplace. Seventy percent of Black babies are born to unwed parents. No question, marriage is not for everyone, but neither is unprotected sex. It's not that being married is the cure for all things messed up, because poverty certainly doesn't magically disappear when two poor folks say "I do." What is important about marriage for Black folks is the demonstration of deep, unconditional respect and love for a person who is giving you the same in return. Some of us are afraid of commitment, others wary of failing as husbands, some legitimately worry about finances, and others simply lack the personal courage needed to break the cycle and marry the person who loves us, who has borne a child with us.

Research shows that Black men take all kinds of crazy risks with our lives. Thousands of us drink too much, smoke too much, have unprotected sex, don't exercise, fail to eat healthy foods, engage in gunplay, seek out fights—all manner of ridiculously risky behavior. The irony is that research also shows that married men

"**70%**
—— OF ALL BLACK BABIES ——
ARE BORN TO UNWED PARENTS."

take far fewer of these kinds of risks. But brothas flee from marriage as if it's Kryptonite and they are Superman. In a collective sense, it seems we have a twisted death wish that requires us to pursue activities that we know will shorten our lives, but run from marriage—the very lifestyle shown to prolong and increase the quality of men's lives—like it's the plague.

Understanding racial and gender oppression are fundamental to becoming men capable of giving and receiving unconditional love and respect for ourselves, each other, and the women and children in our communities. Like Black women, Black men have been subjected to both racial and gender marginalization. An important difference is that throughout our history in America, some Black men have also behaved in ways that diminish opportunity and step on the rights of Black women. We can begin the process of undoing gender oppression starting in our own communities, indeed with our individual selves.

Though all the answers are not clear, it is clear that each of us has agency—the ability to act independently and in our individual and collective best interests—and can choose to use it to hold ourselves and each other accountable for ending words and acts of sexism; disrespect of women; physical violence against women and children; and hateful deeds toward women. We can also support women by standing with them in the fight for women's rights to control their bodies and sexuality; their access to educational opportunities and jobs; fairness in the workplace, including equal pay; parental rights, especially for formerly incarcerated women; and their freedom to love whoever they desire. Standing with Black women also helps heal strained relationships and demonstrates a strong Black masculinity that requires that Black men be present in opposition to gender oppression. Taking such stances will not only advance Black communities but also promises to strengthen Black men.

The effects of fatherlessness in America have been and continue to be well documented in scholarly research, policy debates, and on the *Maury Show*. Though not always obvious, much of the discussion is, at its root, concerned about improving the well-being of children. Fatherhood, as a social issue, is as important as any other single societal priority—including good schools, safe communities, and living-wage jobs. What elevates responsible fatherhood for many people is its relationship to lowering child poverty. The accepted wisdom has been that children need the emotional, financial, and parental guidance of two biological parents. Though this thinking has limitations—it does not apply to all families, for example—we can understand the good intent behind a society pushing for children to have the benefit of both their parents, whenever possible.

For many Black men whose coming of age coincided with the emergence of Hip-hop, the ideal two-parent family has been far from their lived experiences. The essays in this volume recount diverse narratives of Black men who knew their fathers and others who never have; some who are building new Black families to break the cycle, and others not yet

parents; some who well know the inner workings of the child-support-enforcement system, and others hoping to avoid it. What binds the unique experiences told on these pages is a shared cultural experience: Hip-hop. Hip-hop captures—in a mosaic of music, song, dance, art, and language—the political, social, economic, global, familial, and personal dynamics that shaped our lives over the last forty years or so. We are Black men: diverse, masculine, college educated, street educated, straight, gay, fathers, sons, husbands, divorcés, and never-married bachelors. But most importantly for the purposes of this book, we are your brothers, sharing with you a bit of our light from life's lessons and hoping it will help you shine.

■

An Interview with
Davey D.

▶ THERE ARE FEW PEOPLE WHO KNOW AS MUCH ABOUT THE HISTORY
AND CULTURE OF HIP HOP AS JOURNALIST, ACTIVIST, AND MEDIA EXPERT
DAVEY D. TALKING WITH HIM IS LIKE DIVING INTO THE ENCYCLOPEDIAS
OF HIP HOP AND BLACK URBAN CULTURE. HE IS A FORWARD-THINKING
SCHOLAR AND I THOUGHT IT BEST TO HAVE SOMEONE WITH HIS SCOPE OF
KNOWLEDGE AND WISDOM TO ILLUMINATE SOME OFT-OVERLOOKED
PERSPECTIVES ON THIS TOPIC. HE HAS BEEN A FATHER FIGURE IN HIS OWN
HOUSEHOLD AND WITHIN HIS OWN COMMUNITY. HE IS RESPECTED FOR
HIS CUTTING-EDGE, UNAPOLOGETIC ANALYSIS AND HIS ABILITY TO CONNECT
DOTS THAT MOST PEOPLE CAN'T EVEN SEE—A PERFECT FOUNDATION
FOR SETTING UP THE CONTEXT OF THESE COLLECTED WORKS.

ARS: In the simplest, most basic terms, what is your concept of fatherhood? Talk about the difference between being a biological and a practical, more engaged father.

Davey D: Well as a father, I think it's a biological connection. But it's also a spiritual and social connection in the sense that you're charged with rearing and guiding and protecting your family and your children, your offspring.

Fatherhood, in my perspective, means that once you become an adult, fully aware of the responsibilities that entail raising young minds that are easily influenced and are often targeted by outside forces, who don't necessarily have our best interests, then you're part of fatherhood.

So I would consider myself a part of that because my job is to step to those forces that I feel would undermine the type of value systems and the type of upbringing that a lot of people in our community would want to instill in their kids. So whereas I might not be raising your kid or raising a child, I'm going to be stepping to the radio station that undermines the values that you're instilling.

I believe firmly in the concept "it takes a village." The way I ideally see it is I would like to be able to tell a parent, "You don't worry about it. You go and raise your kids and do the best that you can and leave those of us who don't necessarily have kids of our own to fight off the onslaught of attacks that come upon us in social and political circles."

ARS: Is your job any harder as a father figure or is it any easier because of the way Hip-hop is today?

Davey D: I think Hip-Hop today, because its music and culture that is enjoyed by a lot of people of my generation (and is definitely enjoyed by people of the younger generation), allows for us to have shared experiences and to be around the proverbial campfire, so to speak. This allows for lots of teaching moments for young kids. You can use language and references that they can easily understand.

So, when I was coming up and somebody wanted to talk to me about sex or wanted to talk to me about social issues, I mean, you really had to make this leap because what I might have been into was not always necessarily the same thing my parents were into. But nowadays, I could can sit down and watch a Soulja Boy video and pull a young kid aside and say "Let's talk about this," and find out why he likes the dance and what it is that is appealing to him about Soulja Boy, and also be hip enough and sharp enough to go, "Do you know the lyrics to that song?" And we can talk about those lyrics and have a conversation about speaking to women outside their names and about how do we perceive them and treat them and reference them.

That, I think, is an opportunity that Hip-Hop has afforded us. Seeing Jay-Z or other artists that have googobs of money being flashed in a video is an opportunity to put forth the teaching moment about economics, about material gain versus something that is more spiritually centered. So, this is the a topic and there is are all sorts of things under the sun that allow us to have these conversations with young kids. The responsibilities that I have as a father figure, and even as a father, is to stay up on these things.

And I think because we are into Hip-Hop, it's a little bit easier for me to make the leap to what somebody is coming up on and finds attractive versus maybe what I received from past generations. My parents couldn't get into Hip-Hop. It was so foreign to them. It was so removed from where they were coming from. There were no words for it. There was no calculation, no relationship whatsoever. Here, whether I like Soulja Boy or Slim Thug or whoever happens to be hot, is irrelevant because they are speaking a language that I know. So I really get into the conversation and I can, more importantly, easily monitor the type of things that are being sold to young minds.

ARS: There's a prevailing thought that in the absence of fathers, hip-hop raised some of its boys to men. That young men turned to hip-hop culture because they were sort of growing up simultaneously with this new culture that was making its way in the world. And some say hip-hop raised them. Would you agree?

Davey D: I think it did that early on. I mean it did for me. I mean as I was graduating from [high] school in the Bronx, I was pretty much on my own. My family went through a tragic breakup, an unfortunate one, which resulted in my mom moving out to California and me staying in New York.

ARS: So, who raised you?

Davey D: Well, I was raised by my parents. My stepfather and my mom, but they broke up; they had a tragic breakup, which meant that my mom had to bounce out to Cali. I had no idea where my stepfather was and my real dad wasn't a presence in my life for years prior to that. My last year—the last year-and-a-half [of high school], I was in New York pretty much on my own, I mean I stayed with my grandparents. But that was pretty much on my own. It wasn't like my grandparents could really do much for me; they were elderly.

But the point is that living in the Soundview section of the Bronx, every temptation in the world was there. I had friends who had the guns. I had friends who went to jail for murder. I had friends who were drug dealers, who had drugs. All the things that the inner city had to offer, I was around. But I can proudly say that I've never smoked, I've never sold, never been arrested.

And even though I've been exposed and around that a lot, I think the upbringing by my folks laid the foundation, and my involvement with hip-hop fortified that, because my activities were spent crafting my skills as an MC, and my community was my crew: TDK Crew out of Co-op City, and then later the Avengers over in the Marble Hill section.

Going over to my people's houses, and instead of getting into trouble, I'm trying to perfect rhymes. Instead of running around trying to be a hard rock, as we used to call it in those days, I was trying to figure out how to get on the mic at a gig. My pen and my pad were my salvation.

I mean, I just was showing somebody writings that I did as far back as '78, and when I look at them, they're hard-hitting. They're very emotional. They touch the soul. And some of them were journal entries, and a lot of them were rhymes, books of rhymes, that I just wrote. And so, to me, it was a salvation. I mean, there were many lonely nights in New York City that I had because I didn't have the family, and I was still trying to go through the trauma of the breakups and the way that it went down, which was just terrible.

But making rhymes was the saving grace, and that's what kept me on point. And once I moved out to California I went through the homesickness, because the world was a much larger place. You didn't have MTV and national media that spoke in our language, that connected us from coast to coast, so California culture was very, very different than New York culture.

ARS: What year was this, Davey D, that you moved to California?

Davey D: In '81. Talking about the early '80s. Now, in terms of raising me, I wouldn't say that Hip-Hop raised me into manhood, per se, because I'm coming out of an era where I think there were still a lot of strong Black males around to serve as examples.

They were still Black Pride, Black Power–type brothers. So manhood wasn't going to be easily defined by, at that time, Melle Mel or the Treacherous Three, or what have you. Seeing power being executed and wanting to be in that position, I think the closest would have come with been being around Afrika Bambaataa of the Black Spades, and then later Zulu Nation. Seeing that type of power was always attractive. So, that would even be a model unto itself, like, "How can I be like Bam?" You know what I mean? "How can I be like a Gentle King?" Somebody who yields power, has a crew that's hella deep, and just sick with it. But at the same time, Bam himself, who I've seen a lot and lived around his neighborhood, he didn't necessarily carry himself like that, but he was definitely somebody you weren't going to roll up on. And he was feared. Think about where Bam is coming out of, the whole Malcolm X, Nation of Islam, that whole tradition, you know what I mean?

And one of the often overlooked and not often talked about secrets is that a lot of those pioneers and a lot of those people who are in leadership (so it is not just limited to the pioneers) fell victim to . . . heroin or other drugs . . . in particular angel dust and cocaine (freebasing). And that is something that a lot of people aren't very proud of, especially if they came out of it and escaped it. But it is a legacy that was part of the ruthless attacks that took place on eliminating Black manhood and Black leadership out of the community.

It started off with very vicious attacks, and often fatal attacks, on the Panthers and SNCC and other militant Black leaders who, up to that point, had redefined Black manhood for us. And it actually moved us from being Negroes to being Black; it put a fear into white folks and let an oppressive society know that we will turn around and put a foot in your ass if you keep fucking with us. So manhood became something that today we might call hypermasculinity. It was defined by movies like *Nigger Charley*, *The Return of Nigger Charley*, *Superfly*, and other movies with actors like Jim Brown and Fred Williamson, and all those guys who were strong Black men. You see them in the Colt 45 commercials and all that. They redefined Black manhood, and as a kid you picked up on and you saw those types of figures.

Now, you saw that was being eliminated throughout the '70s and by the time you come into adulthood in the '80s and what have you, you look around and you see that a lot of those pioneering figures who are closer to you, are hooked on drugs and just out of it and just not quite there. They weren't the leaders. So a very interesting thing emerged, and this is something I talked with Chuck D about a long time ago, is that by the time you get to the golden era [of hip hop], the kid brother is now actually the head of the household. And by that what I mean is that his older brother was out for the count for a while. His older brother got caught up. If he didn't get caught up on the heroin epidemic, then a lot of the older brothers got caught up in the crack era, which came right after the heroin and cocaine era which maybe was a five-year window. So you are talking about being a drug abuser all the way up to '78, maybe '77 and then that disappearing, and then by '82, '83, you got the crack era jumping off.

What I'm saying is that there were a lot of elders . . . who got caught up in that. And what it meant was if you came up after that, you saw that. And if you were smart enough . . . not to get caught up in it, you eventually saw yourself coming into the golden era of rap being pretty much the head of the class; meaning that you didn't have the older brother or father figure to look to and go, "Which way do I go, how do I do this?"

Many people weren't around, and as young men we had to kind of find our own way. We were the ones who were going to be blazing the trails by the time that golden era came into play. So for me to see somebody like a Chuck D, who I saw as an older brother . . . was a blessing because it sounded like they were was somebody else who could take those blows first.

So all of a sudden that Afrocentric manhood definition that many of us were starting to really step into, all of a sudden it found itself in competition with an enhanced and a very well-backed definition of manhood as defined by being a thug and a gangster, using. It used the music as a modeling tool, but not without necessarily letting people know that this image is being backed by hundreds and thousands and maybe millions of dollars to project that image. So I don't know if I am making sense, but . . .

ARS: No, you are.

Davey D: In the early '90s, you all of a sudden had where you can do this black power Afrocentric thing or you could do this whole "gangster thug" thing. And if you remember, and I remember it very clearly, by '92, '93, you started to hear people, our younger brothers who were coming up—that black power stuff had played out.

ARS: Enter Bad Boy [Entertainment].

Davey D: And I often wonder where that was coming from. Part of it was that younger generation going through the crack era and seeing their older brothers being strung out and their fathers and mothers being strung out. So they lost a lot of respect for [their] elders.

For example, and I will just use this as a microcosm to illustrate the larger picture: Coming out of that golden era where you have maybe people that are coming up and getting manhood kind of defined by the Afrocentric messages that are coming out of 5 Percent, Nation of Islam, all that stuff. It gets replaced by, or gets redefined by, gangster rap. Because gangster rap was always there, but to have having it just totally be, have the Black Power stuff eliminated, and the gangster rap just on the stage by itself, with the full backing of corporations, created this situation where you had two types of manhood: you could go this way, or you could go that way.

Now, at the same time you also have the rise of these talk shows, and I don't know if you recall Ricki Lake, Maury Povich. Jerry Springer came a little bit later, but there were all these early talk shows where for the first time, you saw folks from the hood just being put up onstage, with no checks or balances. You know, you saw folks just sitting up there with all the stereotypical mannerisms that you would never expect to see on TV. The "wild child" type of situation being put out there, with talk show hosts that routinely would say: "You know, stepping up to your parents, putting them out their misery, so to speak, is the norm." In other words, it became kind of fashionable to be disrespectful to your elders, and to talk down on them, and to look down on them. I mean, is this making sense, what I'm saying?

ARS: Yup.

Davey D: So what you had was outside forces, who now had a seat in our community because of their connection with this Hip-Hop thing, especially the more gangster side which they vicariously lived through, now suddenly offering opinions and assessments on how we, as a community, should be. You know, part of that was, like, "Fuck these elders! Who cares about Bambaataa?" To see, all of a sudden, that KRS-One can't get his record on the radio or to have to go to white [radio] program directors to beg to get your record on, and you're talking the Black Power stuff, is really demoralizing.

ARS: Right, right.

Davey D: And then to turn around and to see like it: "Well damn, look at these gangster cats, they just rolled up there and got their shit on." You have manhood being redefined for a younger generation.

So, our challenge [now] is for a lot of people who came out of that golden era—who are now thirty, forty years old—to see how they can . . . take charge, be in position where they can hopefully be an example of what manhood should look like, and hopefully fill those expectations that people would have.

Because now, you've got young cats that are looking, and they've been raised on a diet of money, cars, sex, women, thuggism. And you've got to be able to come and say, "Well, I've got something for you." You just can't be like, "I'm still working for somebody, and that person is still kicking my ass at the job," because they're going to be looking at you like, "Well, that's not how Puffy's rolling. That's not how Jigga's rolling. That's not how Mike Jones is rolling, or any of these other people."

So we, hopefully, have laid down the groundwork to have institutions, have learned how to carry ourselves as winners, have positioned ourselves to be saying, "Well, I am the editor of the magazine." No, better yet, "I own the magazine that I'm the editor of. I have a viable business. And more importantly, you will see me, very often, step to a lot of these enemies of our community who are running roughshod over us." And I think that's where we stand now.

And so, kind of going back to the whole thing of fatherhood, it's complicated now, because just raising a kid is hard enough. To raise a kid, and then go these other extra yards—starting your own business, doing all these things—that's just daunting for the average person.

ARS: I think you make some really powerful points. I want to close out and ask you to connect the dots around fatherhood, as it relates to raising girls. So I'm going to put it like this: If you had a *daughter* today, given the state of where women are in the world of hip-hop, how do you think you would approach raising your daughter, if you had one today?

Davey D: I think one of the things that I have personally found as a bachelor who dates a lot and all that is that I think a lot of women have either very skewed ideas of manhood or unrealistic expectations. I think they have a warped sense of what being a man is about.

Most of the women that I have come across just in dating situations, I could probably say safely eight out of ten have been beaten on or have had something traumatic that has happened, which is not unusual. I have a bunch of women friends, and even some of the most intelligent and strong-minded women that I know have been put into these situations.

I don't want my daughter to be seeking out somebody who's reckless in their behavior, but somebody who personifies a willingness to think things through, who has the quiet confidence to know that, even if they come to the party late, that they have enough skill sets and enough resources that they can catch up, so they don't have to try to keep up with the Joneses, because they are the Joneses. They're not trying to work for somebody; they're trying to own the place that they work at. Somebody who understands the importance of God and spirituality, which has also been removed from our definition of manhood.

I think, ultimately, manhood—and fatherhood being an extension of manhood—is somebody who can walk with God, is not afraid to admit it, and is not afraid to acknowledge that God, and therefore will seek guidance and counsel from that spiritual base, which ultimately will govern our behavior and activities.

■

[SIDE A]

LOOK HERE, NOT A THING TO FEAR

BROTHER TO BROTHER NOT ANOTHER AS SINCERE

TEACH A MAN HOW TO BE FATHER

TO NEVER TELL A WOMAN HE CAN'T BOTHER

YOU CAN'T SAY YOU DON'T KNOW

WHAT I'M TALKIN' 'BOUT

BUT ONE DAY . . . BROTHERS GONNA WORK IT OUT

—PUBLIC ENEMY

"BROTHERS GONNA WORK IT OUT"

FEAR OF A BLACK PLANET, 1990

Freestyle Fatherhood

▶ LASANA HOTEP

Being born in 1974 set me on a course to come of age as a person cloaked in the international phenomenon that Afrika Bambaataa would name Hip-hop. Hip-hop as an international youth movement influenced everything from my style of dress to my political views. Its infectious elements of graf writin', deejayin', breakin', emceein', and knowledge called me, initiated me, and sent me back out into the world to live its truth. The two most influential characteristics of Hip-hop in my journey from B-boy to B-man were improvisation and sampling.

Hip-hop, like most African music, has improvisation at its core. The art of improvisation demands one to be so skilled in his/her craft that the lyricist is prepared to perform whenever it's time for a solo. In Hip-hop, we call this freestyle. Sampling is used to take components of previously recorded material to create a new, unique musical piece with an identity unto itself. Hammer's "U Can't Touch This" has an identity independent of Rick James's "Superfreak" although the sampling is obvious. Improvisation and sampling also best describe my perspective on and experience with the phenomenon of fatherhood.

Not having a full grasp of what I was truly facing as a young African man born in Los Angeles, California between the 1965 and 1992 uprisings, I *had* to freestyle. Moving to Long Beach, California at the age of seven where the true threat of gangbangin' loomed over me, also required me to freestyle. Relocating from California to Texas while in high school and adjusting to life in the South demanded more freestyle. During my escape from a life of disappoint-

ment and powerlessness into a life of courage and empowerment, I had to spit like freestyle legend Supernatural. During these different stages in my life, the one constant was my loving, supportive, and courageous mother, Kim Stone. The fatherhood component was more of a group effort with samples from various pieces.

The most consistent element of fatherhood came from my biological father, Lawrence Garrett Silas, Sr. My father and mother were a young couple—aged twenty-two and nineteen, respectively—who found themselves in love and with a child. After I turned four, the relationship ended. The deal breaker

was my father's substance-abuse problem. He used many chemicals to self-medicate, but the most destructive was the "hip-hop"

▸ [Lasana's uncle (left), Lasana's father (middle), and Lasana (right)]

drug, crack. My father eventually became so consumed by his addictions that he eventually ended up living on LA's Skid Row. He has recently recovered, and through it all we remained close and in contact.

My father set the foundation for the kind of intellectual man I have become. From him I inherited compassion, an unquenchable thirst for knowledge, and critical thinking. He lived with my great-grandmother, Big Mama, before he ended up on Skid Row. In the summer, I would visit him and Big Mama. During my visit in 1984, I received a phone call from my mother notifying me of the death of my younger cousin, Glen. He had drowned in a lake during the July 4 holidays. Glen was only seven; I was devastated. I remember my father being there to console me as I dealt with such an enormous loss as a child.

My father, drug addict and all, read the newspaper every morning. As a matter of fact, he read and still reads whatever he can get his hands on. I attribute my love of reading to him. My father is the epitome of independent study. He has no high school diploma but is well versed on topics as varied as sports history and world politics. Not only does he read, he is a critical thinker.

Even when I was a child he would talk to me like an adult about various topics and offer his analysis and ask for my perspective. Every subject had to be put into historical context. We couldn't talk about the NBA without mentioning its merging with the ABA and the role it played in the style of the game. There was no discussion of Ronald Reagan as president of the United States without mentioning his role as governor of California and the targeting of the Black Panthers. Lawrence Silas, Sr., despite his personal challenges, demonstrated the power of a freethinking man.

Another contributor to my concept of fatherhood and manhood was my mother's younger brother, Uncle Craig. Craig lived life on the edge because he thought that he would meet the fate of his two older brothers, Larry and Barry, and die by the age of twenty-two. His belief led him to adopt a reckless lifestyle that landed him in the penitentiary throughout a large portion of his life. After his first long stint in prison, Craig came to live with my mother, my brother, and me for a short while. Ironically, Craig's personal life, while riddled with irresponsibility, had no bearing on him showing me how to be responsible.

He encouraged me to do well in school and to stay out of trouble as a way for my mother to have peace of mind. He also offered me my first lessons on healthy eating, something young men are not often taught. While in prison, he embraced Islam and brought back Muslims' disdain for pork. I too adopted this contempt for "the other white meat" and expunged it from my diet at age thirteen. This was the first of many dietary adjustments I would make toward wellness. Just as important, he taught me how to sweep, mop, vacuum, and iron creases into my pants. All of these skills allowed me to be more of an asset to the family and I came to understand that domestic work is not only for women.

Another uncle, my father's brother, helped mold me by being an example of stability. Uncle Cuffy was married, took care of his children, and owned his home. This was an anomaly in my immediate circle of men. He provided me with a glimpse of a life outside of the prescribed gangbangin' track of most Southern California youth. He also had a great career. He worked as an editor in television news and sometimes he'd take me to CBS with him and let me see how television "works." This exposure led me to work in television while in college and work as an associate news producer for an NBC affiliate after earning my degree. I did not work in television news long, but seeing this successful Black man in a predominantly white industry allowed me to see options I would not have known existed.

Toward the closing of the golden era of Hip-hop, the early 1990s, I began to make the transition into manhood. Two distinct masculine forces shaped me during this period of my life. One was Black conscious rap music provided by the likes of Public Enemy, Poor Righteous Teachers, Boogie Down Productions/KRS-One, Brand Nubian, Def Jef, Big Daddy Kane, Kool Moe Dee, X-Clan, and the Jungle Brothers. These musicians and the music they produced sparked my interest in African history and culture, which ultimately led to me making the empowerment of African people throughout the Diaspora my life's work.

The second influential male force in my life during the golden era was my mother's new husband, Louis Turner. My stepfather and I have not seen eye-to-eye on most things in life. However, I want to acknowledge his impact on my concept of fatherhood. His being willing to marry my mother—a single woman with two sons—and providing food, clothing, and shelter for us as if we were his own, is a testament to fatherhood and manhood. We have maintained contact despite our differences and his divorce from my mother because I respect him as a man and he respects the man that I have become.

My journey from B-boy to B-man has had its tragedies and triumphs. I have had to rely on my ability to freestyle to negotiate the streets, navigate through the university, and nurture my marriage. My perceptions of manhood and fatherhood have evolved as I have analyzed the samples from the various men who have fathered me throughout my life. As my wife and I plan our family, I have the benefit of all of the wisdom gained from my father figures and the impact of the freestyles of their lives.

■

What Is a Man?

THE FOLLOWING EXCERPT IS TAKEN FROM KEVIN POWELL'S 2003 BEST-
SELLING ESSAY COLLECTION *WHO'S GONNA TAKE THE WEIGHT? MANHOOD, RACE,
AND POWER IN AMERICA*. KEVIN POWELL INTERVIEWED TUPAC SHAKUR ON
SEVERAL OCCASIONS WHILE HE WAS A SENIOR WRITER AT *VIBE* MAGAZINE, AND
WROTE WHAT ARE WIDELY CONSIDERED THE DEFINITIVE ARTICLES AND
PROFILES ON THE LATE TUPAC SHAKUR.

▸ KEVIN POWELL

I met Tupac's natural father, Billy Garland, a few weeks after Tupac
died. Tupac had been so adamant about not knowing his father
that I did not believe that this man was in fact his father until I saw
him in person. But the moment I saw him, I knew he was: There
was the tall, lean body, the flat-footed walk, the girlish eyelashes,
the long nose, and, yeah, the bushy eyebrows. To be honest, I had
mixed feelings about the meeting. While I was glad to meet this
man Afeni Shakur had referred to in my first *Vibe* article on Tupac
as "Billy," I thought of how long it took Billy to reconnect with his
son. And that was only after he had seen Tupac in *Juice*. What, I
wondered, would have been different about Tupac's life had Billy
been there? What would have been the same? Did Billy only become interested in his son once he became famous and, presumably,
rich? Did Billy realize Tupac had spent his entire twenty-five years
searching for father figures in the form of teachers, street hustlers,

> **"There had been no blueprint for Billy Garland, just as there had been no blueprint for Tupac Shakur, or for me, for that matter."**

fellow rappers like Ice-T and Chuck D, and men as different as Suge Knight and Quincy Jones? I didn't ask Billy Garland any of these questions, but they were definitely on my mind. No matter: I sat and talked with Billy Garland for two or three hours in his Jersey City apartment, about his life, about Tupac's life, and about his absence from Tupac's universe. Billy showed me pictures of himself with Tupac, of the letters 'Pac had written him from prison, of the many cards he had received since Tupac's untimely death. Tupac had barely known this man, I thought, just as I barely knew my father. Was Billy Garland one of those Black men I had described previously, one of the damaged souls from the civil rights era, an ex-Panther and now a broken-down warrior trying to get a grip on his life via his dead son? Billy even asked me if he should sue Afeni Shakur for half of the Tupac Shakur estate. I was both astounded and appalled. This man had really been nothing more than a drop of sperm, and now he wanted to reap the benefits of the money a dead rapper as iconic as Tupac was sure to bring. But for some reason I was not angry with Billy Garland. A part of me understood exactly where he was coming from because, hell, he is a Black man in America and he has nothing to show for it except a tiny apartment, and a dead, famous son. Billy had had a hard life himself, in the 1970s and 1980s, as he struggled to come of age as Tupac was coming of age. There had been no blueprint for Billy Garland, just as there had been no blueprint for Tupac Shakur, or for me, for that matter. We were—are—simply thrown out there and told to swim, although most of us do not know how and are too terrified to learn.

But it is something to see older Black men as I do, as a man myself. I will be completely candid here and say that I have carried around a great deal of resentment toward older Black men since my father disowned me when I was eight years old. Indeed, I have had little tolerance, little respect, and very little interest in what most of them have to say for themselves. It is the worst form of cowardice to bring a child into the world and then abandon that child either because you cannot cope or because you and the child's mother are not able to get along. How many Black boys and Black girls have had their emotional beings decimated by that father void? Certainly Tupac, and certainly me.

Perhaps it is for this reason that I cannot readily recall all that Billy Garland said to me on that day after he asked my advice about suing Afeni Shakur. I was disgusted and saw in him my father and my grandfather and my uncle, my mother's only brother, and undeniably I saw myself and what I could possibly become. The predictability horrified me, because I could hear the echoes of my mother's caveat from my childhood: *Don't be like your father.* But what did my mother mean, precisely? If not like him, then like whom? In seeking to raid Tupac's grave for dollars, Billy Garland was showing the worst attributes of Black manhood, but also of White manhood, of American manhood. So what would the alternative be? How does one break the vicious cycle, begun on the plantations, of Black man as stud, as Black male body forced to tend someone else's land and property, as Black man torn away from his family, moved to and fro, of Black man being beaten down to the point that his woman and his children no longer know his name. Again, what of slavery, which lasted 246 years and lingers still in the collective bosom of Black men in America, particularly since we were slaves a hundred years longer than we have been free? So how could I really be mad at Billy Garland—or my father, for that matter—anymore? Garland, via Tupac's death, was getting more attention than he had ever gotten in his entire rotten life and he needed Tupac's death to validate his existence. How twisted a concept! But it is true. And what of my father, that no-good do-for-nothing, as my mother often referred to him? I may never see the man again in my lifetime, don't care to, really, but I know wherever he is, he is not free. He is wounded; he is, like an older Black men and like a lot of younger Black men, in a state of arrested development, suspended above the fiery coals of his unstable journey here in America. But, with all of my being, I have to muster the nerve to forgive him, my father, for impregnating my mother, for not being there at the hospital when I was born, for not marrying my mother and leaving her to the whims of the welfare agency, for only showing up sporadically the first eight years of my life, for declaring to my mother on that damp, rainy day that she had lied to him, that I was not his child, that he would not give her a "near-nickel" for me ever again—and he has not. Oh, how I suffered, as Tupac suffered, without a male figure in my life, someone whose skin felt like mine, whose blood beat like mine, whose walk pounded the earth for answers, like mine. But alas, poor Tupac, it was not meant to be, and you are dead, and I am here, and we both have fathers, yet we both are also fatherless. The only thing I can say at this moment in my life journey—because, unlike Tupac, I did get to make it past twenty-five, into my thirties—is that I have to stay alive any way I can, and I have to be my own father now.

Baba

▶ LUMUMBA AKINWOLE-BANDELE

Trying to avoid being late for Saturday morning dance class at Ifetayo, my daughters and I trot down Church Avenue. We stop at a light, I bend down to fix a ponytail, and I hear the women next to me say to her friend, "He is such a great father." To most men this statement may sound flattering. After hearing this for the umpteenth time I finally realize why it bothers me. The strangers who offer this compliment, simply from seeing me with my children, know very little and assume plenty. Too often my mere presence with my children meets the ultimate criteria of being "a great father." What if I am abusive or neglectful? The realities of young Black men cause us to have a very short measuring stick for healthy and great fathers. And we know those realities all too well, almost as if they are songs in heavy rotation on Hot 97: fatherlessness and criminalization, along with inadequate housing, education, employment, and health care—which all stem from the

twin towers of capitalism and racism. They continue to be unshak-

"Hip Hop able shadows for young Black men. So for most in our com-
munity, they are happy if a father is simply present.

As young Black men in the late 1970s and early '80s struggled to find their way, many found a home in Hip Hop. After consistently being told what we weren't, we were able to define ourselves. The issues mentioned, while

has always
real, were not the things that defined us. We were so much more and we used Hip Hop as a way of expressing what and who we were.

Hip Hop has always reflected the current conditions of our people. And beyond what is obvious, there is a new sound

reflected the current to Hip Hop—a new feel and
a new understanding. For many of us, our approaches to our lives, especially fatherhood, have developed as well. We have moved beyond basic gender roles and are attempting to parent in a way that develops our children in a far more effective way. As a DJ, I recognize that my tolerance for music that I wouldn't want my children to hear has diminished greatly. Although I rarely spin for the "top
conditions 40" crowd I occasionally get an R. Kelly request. My instant response
is always "hell no." My politics have become far more personal.

My politics come from growing up as a child in The East (a Black Nationalist educational and cultural institution in Central Brooklyn). I was surrounded
by men who were, for

of our people."
the most part, present in their families' lives. These men served as positive, strong male role models for most of the children. The men

I knew growing up were strong, defiant, courageous, and proud. It was these images that helped me put on "my face" for the world. However, as we know, the African-centered male image of the 1970s was one that was rooted firmly in machismo and supported most basic patriarchal traditions.

This face that I was preparing would not be radically different than that of my peers not in The East. The core pillars of most Black men's understanding of manhood were to be strong, nonemotional, and firm. These images of masculinity were reaffirmed for us through mass media and most importantly through our folktales and rap music. The characters that were born out of the imagination of the emcee became the lives young people attempted to mirror.

Baba, which means father in several African languages including Yoruba, Arabic and Kiswahili, Adeyemi "Yemi" Bandele was not only present in our family but also involved in my life. I guess it also helped that I was actively involved in his. The joy of my childhood evenings and weekends was being by his side as he went to meetings. His work focused on organizing against apartheid in South Africa, the police killing of Arthur Miller, the invasion of Grenada, and coordinating the African Street Carnival. Much of my joy simply came from being at Baba's side. It didn't take me long to realize that having a father in my home was a rare thing for young men my age. Most of the adult males present on the block were uncles and grandfathers.

At an early age I learned what a tremendous impact that support makes on children. For most of the major benchmarks in my life I contemplated how Baba would feel about it. I have always had problems with critiques, constructive or otherwise. Baba's opinion was the only one I was really concerned about. For example, I was threatened with suspension from high school for conducting "direct actions" as part of organizing for an African history class. Baba came to school and defended me. The level of empowerment I felt that day was tremendous and it greatly informed (albeit subconsciously) my approach on parenting.

On February 14, 1999, at about two in the morning, my wife Monifa gave birth to our first daughter, Naima. I was twenty-seven years old. My father was twenty-one when he had his first child. I figured if he was able to do it at twenty-one, I surely could do it at twenty-seven. Immediately after I turned thirty, Monifa gave birth to our second daughter, Adasa. My life changed from being focused on the late-night political meetings to laying out clothes and lunch for my girls.

Baba had said to me at a very early age that being a father wasn't easy. That was an understatement. The easy part was the first stages of late-night feedings and diaper changes. The hard part was and is trying to prepare our children to live in, transform, and improve this world.

Being physically present is a logical necessity for being a father; however, our children need and deserve much more. My measuring stick for being a good father was based on experiences with my father and other fathers in my community. My job as a father is "to love," which means to be present, to be involved, to listen, to challenge, and to share. The idea that I am responsible for developing a healthy human being is overwhelmingly frightening, but the idea of my child being left to figure out life along the way or to allow others to attempt to do it is far more frightening and unimaginable for me.

Half of the time I'm playing catch-up trying to understand what's going on, but at the end of the day Naima and Adasa both know when they turn around I will be standing right there. My daughters have a way of exposing my issues and characteristics. This continues to be unnerving, but is necessary for my personal development as well as my children's. I was/am forced to acknowledge that the patriarchal environment that I grew up in did impact me greatly.

For most of my adult life I embraced most mainstream anti-sexist ideologies. Now I am faced with the reality of raising two daughters in a dangerous world—one that destroys girls in ways I never imagined. My ideology was not enough. I had to figure out how I was going to shield them from these things and also prepare them to counter it. First, I had to acknowledge and change some things about myself. I had to realize that while I supported the

destruction of patriarchy as an institution, I did not approach it
with the level of seriousness or urgency like I have with capitalism,
racism, and colonialism.

The amount of support Baba gave me throughout my life had to
be tripled with my girls. There was no African-centered institution
to thoroughly insulate and prepare them culturally and politically
for this world. I don't have all the answers, but I am going to find
them and do the best I can.

Being a healthy father isn't something that is done in isolation. The best fathers I know are involved and attached to communities. They are in circles that encourage the healthy development of families, which simply means being in the company and lives of other families and fathers that are trying to do the same thing. These circles become not only a resource of information on parenting, but also a physical and psychological support base when you need it.

I have surrounded myself with some of the best fathers I know. Thank-you to the brothers that I learn from. I continue to be enriched through our conversations, our mutual experiences, and by observation. Thank you Baba Malik, Baba Emir, Baba Tarik, Baba Gamba, Baba Atiba, Baba Will, Baba Russell, and plenty others. We aren't perfect, but we are aggressively pursuing perfection.

I've been told on many occasions that I am just like Yemi. Much of this was my intent, while some I had very little control over. Adeyemi Bandele has been and continues to be my measuring stick.

■

Work and Travel

EDITOR'S NOTE: STEVEN G. FULLWOOD'S CONTRIBUTION TO THIS ANTHOLOGY, THANKS
TO RETHA POWERS, IS ONE OF THE MOST IMPORTANT. AS AN OUT GAY BLACK HIP HOP
HEAD, STEVEN'S BODY OF WORK, INCLUDING THIS ESSAY, REMINDS US THAT "LIFE IS
ABOUT CHANGE" AND IS ABOUT FIGHTING FOR THE FREEDOM TO JUST "BE." IN HIS BLOG,
HE WRITES "HIP-HOP, IN ITS MOST PROVOCATIVE FORM, HAS BEEN ABOUT RESISTANCE.
BEEN ABOUT BEING CUTTING EDGE. FRANKLY, YOU CAN'T GET MORE CUTTING EDGE . . .
[THAN] BEING BLACK AND NONHETEROSEXUAL. HIP-HOP'S MISOGYNY AND HYPER-
MASCULINITY HAS DEFINED IT SINCE ITS INCEPTION. SIMPLY BY BEING OUT CHALLENGES
THOSE PARADIGMS, AND INVITES A REEXAMINATION OF WHAT IS MALE AND FEMALE
TO THE WHOLE COMMUNITY. HIP-HOP HAS ALWAYS LAID CLAIM TO THE NOTION THAT IT
WAS KEEPING THINGS REAL. WELL YOU CAN'T GET ANY REALER THAN WHAT I'M
ABOUT, WHICH IS REDEFINING COMMUNITY BY INTERJECTING SOME MUCH NEEDED
COMMENTARY ABOUT THE SEXUAL LIFE OF THE BLACK COMMUNITY AS WE KNOW IT.
MANY BLACK HETEROSEXUAL FOLK WOULD RATHER BE SEEN AS THE MODEL
FOR LIFE AS OPPOSED TO BEING IN THE CONTINUUM. WELL, THEY AIN'T AND THEY WILL
NEVER BE." CASE CLOSED.

WHAT FOLLOWS IS A HEARTWARMING STORY ABOUT A FATHER AND SON WHO BOTH
SEEK TO MATTER IN THE WORLD, VIA THEIR OWN MEANS, ON THEIR OWN TERMS.

▸ STEVEN G. FULLWOOD

I rarely saw my father simply sitting and resting. I always saw him sleeping on the couch, resting between the two or more jobs he always and proudly held—shoes off, knees slightly bent, his large back to the rest of the world. There was never a time in my lifetime when my father did not work. It was common for my father to come home after 3 PM and be on his way out the door before 5 PM. In the few moments we had him, my siblings and I would bother him for attention, money, or both. He generally complied. Daddy's main lesson to me was that I could always work—if I were willing. I came from him.

He came from and was the namesake of two Stevens before him, his father and his grandfather. A 1940s Southern boy, young Steve lived on a farm in Arkansas. He was accustomed to getting up early to work long hours in the fields under the watchful gaze of his father, a stern man who later in his life became a fiery minister who was known for taking no mess.

Farm life was no joke. Daddy and his siblings spent a great deal of their formative years helping to plant and raise tobacco, corn,

▶ [Steven, deep in thought]

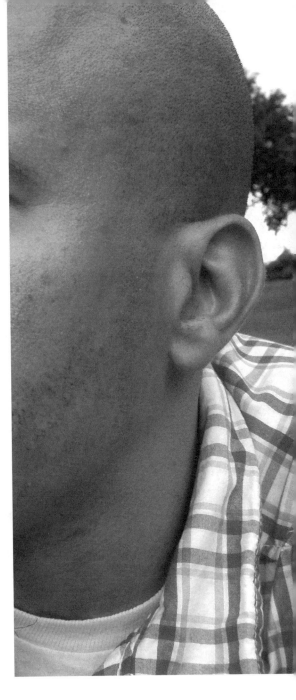

and whatever else the family needed. After graduating high school, the seventeen year-old hopped a train to Ohio, where he met a woman named Elaine, married her, and the couple settled down to raise three girls and two boys—one of which was me.

As a child I didn't like him, and I didn't think he liked me. I always thought my father wanted a more masculine son than I turned out to be. This painful fact was confirmed many times over. One Sunday I came home after church to find my father waiting for me. I remember him taking me by the shoulder, pointing me toward a window leading to our backyard.

"Stevie, do you know that your so-called friends sat on our back porch and talked about you like a dog?" he asked. Like them, he accused me of being antisocial, and claimed that I thought that I was better than them. Well, he was half right. I was antisocial because I simply didn't know how to connect with boys my age besides playing sports. More importantly, I was too busy trying to hide my erection.

But it was the disappointment on his face that tore me up. He wasn't upset with them— he was upset with me. *I* wasn't social. *I* wasn't hanging out with my friends. *I* had the problem. So instead of defending me, he sided with some silly boys who he wouldn't give a second thought to except as barometers to his flaming son's behavior. By sixteen, I was having a hard time adopting the "hang out on the corner and wait for what" paradigm that had ensnared so many of my peers. I knew I was going somewhere, but where?

> **"I will always be in your corner, always, 'till they put me in the ground."**

In 1996 I left Ohio to attend graduate school in Georgia. A year before that I came out to my father. He was the last person I told because I was terrified that he would reject me. He didn't. In fact, his main concern was that I could be hurt for going public with my sexual preference. He told me not to tell anyone, concerned that I could be fired for being out. The very next day my father came to see me at the library where I was working. The tightness in my throat dissolved the moment I saw his face.

In 2005, almost a decade later, I called my father. It was a warm Saturday morning in October, and I was at work. My father and his siblings often caught up with one another early in the morning on weekends, and so I too look forward to catching him during these times.

"I got your postcard," he said.

Two months prior I was vacationing in the Dominican Republic, splashing about in ocean with my now ex-fiancé. Dad brings up the postcard inscribed with the words "Dominican Republic" and, more importantly, "fiancé."

"Man, you always going somewhere. Don't you ever stay in one place?"

My father liked to rib me about my love of travel.

"Don't you know planes are dangerous? *Boy, don't you know that we're at war?*"

Getting on planes wasn't exactly his thing. When speaking about such matters, his voice would go from playful to dead serious. 9/11 had taken its toll on Americans. The attack stripped away the sense of security many people had taken for granted.

Then the U.S. declared war in Iraq. Shortly thereafter, daily papers and broadcast news screamed stories of anti-America sentiment around the world. People were being detained, kidnapped, killed.

Still, it was not enough to keep me off a plane. I live to travel. Too much of the world to see, do, think about. Can't trust anyone to tell me about anywhere. I have to go myself. Daddy knows that. Told him a million times.

"So," I said, "I want you to meet my partner."

Silence.

Then, in a pleading tone, he said, "Man, do I have to?"

"Yes, you have to," I said immediately, feeling brave. But I don't know exactly why I said it. He certainly didn't have to meet my man, particularly if he was going to be an asshole about it.

Then he said something that fucked me the hell up.

"Stevie, listen. I will always be in your corner, always, till they put me in the ground. I will always respect you and what you choose, but I gotta tell you, that ain't my way of life."

"Okay, I know that, Daddy. I'm not saying it has to be," I said.

"See, Stevie, you took the hard road. You could have been the president of the United States, married to a woman with kids. You could have went very far, but instead you took the hard road."

I was sitting at my computer and began typing up my father's words. Something in me said *write this down*. I would need these words later.

I didn't take the hard road, it took me. And millions more. But I didn't say that. Couldn't say it. He continued.

"You say that's the way you are, and that you have to be honest, and it may be selfish of me to want differently. But I was looking forward to seeing three or four Stevies running around in my living room, you know?" He laughed. "But you took the hard road. Maybe you didn't though. It was put on you, and that's just the way it is."

I struggled to get my bearings.

"Daddy, I didn't make myself this way, I just am," I stammer. My face was hot. I wasn't mad, upset, or frustrated. Just filled with wonder.

"Life is about change, Daddy. Black folks would still be enslaved, we could still be in Africa, but we are not. Many of us died on the way coming here. We fought for freedom. We are *still* fighting for freedom. Things have and will continue to change, for the better, I hope. I am a part of that change."

"Look, Stevie, I ain't got much going for me, except for my work. I like to work. I don't know if you've gotten to that age, but for me, it keeps me out of things that I don't want to necessarily be involved in at this point. You know what I mean?"

Now it was time for me to be silent.

"I want someone to know that I was here and that I mattered. So if I die next week, go looking around the house, there will be pieces of paper with what I thought and how I lived, what I did," he said.

Then, his tone changed and so did the conversation.

"You know how hard it is to write. It doesn't come sometimes. If it doesn't come easy, then it ain't writing. Sometimes the thoughts are really clear, that's when the writing comes."

Here. This is where I was going. To share a small story about my beautiful father who has a story that is more than the sum of what he said or did. Complex. This is the man I met as an adult.

He changes the subject again. "I look forward to the weekends because I get to see the grandkids," Dad says, "which is good since I can't look at you."

"When I come to visit, Dad, give me your stuff. I'll make sure people know what you did."

■

"THE GHETTO'S BEEN GOOD TO ME, WANTED RIGHT FOR MY LIFE EVEN

THOUGH WHAT THEY HAD WAS WRONG. THE GHETTO'S BEEN GOOD TO ME,

TEACHING ME HOW TO HOLD ON, BE STRONG FIND A WAY TO KEEP ON."

—OpTimUs, "THE GHETTO'S BEEN GOOD TO ME"

Love, Lessons, Learning, and Leadership

▶ TIMOTHY DAVID JONES, a.k.a. OpTimUs

I look back fondly on my upbringing in the housing projects of East New York, Brooklyn. My environment then, along with hip-hop, included me in its blended family. The family values that I learned early on from hip-hop taught me unconditional love and helped me to be a father in my own blended family today.

I grew up in a family of five boys and I am the youngest. My father was in the house until I was about ten or eleven. During adolescence I was blessed to be fathered by men who guided me with wisdom and purpose throughout my life. Men such as Jeremiah Jones (who headed the youth center in my projects) and the brothers who, despite their life choices, knew right from wrong and steered me away from the mistakes that they made.

I also came to know the blessings of family life through the positive influence of hip-hop. The music and the culture served as a bond that formed many relationships. This new phenomenon called hip-hop served as the rationale to put differences and personal agendas to the side in an effort to be a part of something that was bigger than the individual. Hip-hop encouraged individuals to form the positive family bonds that previously were presented to inner-city youth in the form of gangs. In fact, the most renowned MCs were parts of groups or crews: LL Cool J was partnered with DJs Bob Cat and Cut Creator; Rakim with Eric B; KRS-One with Scott LaRock and Boogie Down Productions; Queen Latifah with the Flavor Unit; Chuck D with Public Enemy; Scarface with the Geto Boys; Ice Cube with NWA; and Big Daddy Kane with Mr. Cee and the Juice Crew, just to name a few. Whether they intended to or not, all of these groups promoted the value of (and need for) strong family ties.

I carried this perspective throughout my college years and it helped me form a family bond with a group of friends I consider brothers to this day. We created our own standards of manhood and look out for each other constantly: We attend each other's weddings, celebrate the birth of our children, and so on. In college, I was blessed to have another strong connection with a man who guided me into adulthood. He continues to be a strong father figure in my life today. Dr. Barron H. Harvey was the man who fathered me while, in my head, I was having conversations with my biological dad that now remind me of one of lyrics by Lupe Fiasco: *"I want you to be a father / I'm your little boy and you don't even bother / like "brother" without the R."* My relationship with my dad had eventually became nonexistent to the point where I would wonder: *"You see what my problem is? That I don't know where my poppa is."* Those were the thoughts in my head that laid heavy on my heart as I transitioned into adulthood, despite the father figures in my life.

As a young adult, with my personal and professional lives ahead of me, I met Mr. Mahmood "Billo" Harper. Mahmood invited me into his

▸ [Tim, his wife, and their children]

> **"I knew that the success of my marriage would be based on my ability to keep my promises to my wife and my new daughter."**

world and I saw in him a futuristic interpretation of myself as a "Hip-Hop Dad." Mahmood showed me how to incorporate my love of hip-hop into my business and family life.

Within hip-hop culture, the crews evolved similar to how relationships develop in personal life. Rappers went from coming together to do shows and songs to coming together to establish businesses. This shift is exemplified in the emergence of Wu-Tang Clan in 1994. Wu-Tang redefined how to do business within hip-hop. The family structure of "the posse" was a new model. Hip-hop evolved from having crews on the street corner to having clans in the corner office . . . similar to how relationships can evolve from boyfriend/girlfriend status to a husband-and-wife union. As hip-hop continued to develop in this way, so did I. In 1998, I put aside my boyhood ways and got married. I became a husband and a father in the same moment because my wife, Vanessa, had a seven-year-old daughter.

Raising my daughter Jasmine (I never use the term "step") called forth all the positive images and lessons that were presented to me by hip-hop and by the wise men in my life— both my elders and my peers. I was now initiated into a new sort of hip-hop crew. Within my new family, some of hip-hop's basic values and practices applied: nothing should break down the unit, posses roll deep, and your word is your bond. And if someone in the crew presents an "outsider" (i.e., me, in this case) as being "down," then the so-called outsider must receive the same love and support as every other member of the family . . . regardless of tenure. I joined Vanessa and Jasmine's crew by making my wedding vows to *both* of them. I knew that the success of my marriage would be based on my ability to keep my promises to my wife and my new daughter. Without these rules to live by, I don't think that I would have been psychologically or emotionally equipped to be a father to Jasmine.

By 1999, I was a happily married man in my thirties. I was still a hip-hop head and I began to notice a growing frustration within the hip-hop community—mostly centered on the issue of fatherhood. More and more, rappers began to address the pain caused by fathers' dysfunctional relationships with their children. Though I had forgiven my father for his not being around, I could still relate to this pain. It motivated me to do my best for my daughter and for the young people that I worked with as director of the teen program at Martha's Table (Martha's Table is a prominent nonprofit community-based organization in Washington, D.C.). Many of the teens in my program don't have fathers or father figures in their lives. Through my work, I felt I was answering Quan's hip-hop plea: *"Can we please have a moment for children who got raped or murdered, or trapped in the system who never knew their father, never learned to dream but was guided by drug dealers, killers and crack fiends."* I have established long-lasting bonds with most of the teens in my program over the past twelve years and I saw, once again, the value of the blended family.

Still and all, I longed to have a son. I believed a son would help heal any remaining wounds that were created by my biological father. In 1999, God answered my prayers and my son Isaiah Jeremiah Ezra Jones was born on my thirty-first birthday. He was named in honor of all the father figures who filled in the gaps for me and my wife. Since that day and moving forward, Isaiah will always know what life is like with his dad. His life challenges will not be based on the hard circumstances that come with growing up in a single-parent home. Instead, he will benefit from my having broken a cycle of bitterness and my having learned how to love past pain. The father and the man that I become; and the man that I will raise my son to be, are deeply rooted in my belief, trust, confidence, and reliance on Jesus Christ for all things. As I continued to mature into manhood, I found comfort and joy in serving Jesus Christ in spirit and in truth, in my rewarding work, and in a faithful marriage. All these things helped me to be secure in my identity and purpose in life.

When teens ask why I am the way that I am and why I care as much as I do, I love that I get the chance to tell them that I love them because Jesus first loved me and that He gave me so many fathers to model after. I believe I must be a father for them too. I am also proud to tell them that hip-hop culture, contrary to popular belief, has been a guidepost for me to follow with regard to building a family unit—be that family in the household, in the projects, on the block, or at the local community center. The role that hip-hop has played in my life is based on an insight that was God-given. Hip-hop influences my ministry from the pulpit as a minister and I have been afforded a spiritual father who leads me as my Pastor, Bishop Larry H. Jordan, Sr. I am able to reflect on hip-hop culture in a way that many see as contradictory to how hip-hop has been defined by society. I know better. In the words of Inspector Deck I say, "*Leave it up to me while I be living proof to kick the truth to the young black youth.*" My life with hip-hop, family, mentors, and friends has consisted of the love, lessons, learning, and leadership necessary to mold me into what I am and all the things I will become.

One Love,
OpTimUs
OPportunity and TIMe for US
■

"WE EXPOSE WAYS FOR THE YOUTH TO SURVIVE SOME THINK IT'S

WRONG BUT WE TEND TO THINK IT'S RIGHT SO MAKE ALL THEM ENDS

YOU CAN MAKE, CAUSE WHEN YOU'RE BROKE, YOU BREAK."

—SNOOP DOGG, "LITTLE GHETTO BOYS"

From Education to Get Money: The Challenge of Parenting in and Beyond the Hip-Hop Generation

Unlike the dominant mythology of the hip-hop generation*—
namely the narrative of Black boys with missing fathers raised by
their mothers—I grew up having a healthy relationship with my
father. The pent-up frustration, the tales from the dark side of a
father not being present at critical rites of passage, of being forced
to seek out surrogate fathers in street culture, were not my reality.
And even now as I recall coming of age in the hip-hop generation,
rarely do I think of my parents as separate entities. When it came
to parenting, they were a single unit, and when I think of my father as a parent those are my first memories.

My father was born Samuel Dance in Weeksville, North Carolina, a rural strip of farmland about thirty miles south of the Ches-
apeake Bay. It was an unusually cool weekend in the fall in 1930,
as my grandmother remembered it. Twenty years later, my parents
married. Both my mom and dad were farm laborers. White pota-

toes were a thriving North Carolina industry then. Before automation, the work was done by hand. At the same time, the east end of Long Island, New York, enjoyed a lucrative white potato fall harvest. Every year after the North Carolina July harvest, to make ends meet, my parents migrated to Long Island for work in the fall with a crew of relatives and childhood friends before returning home. It was 1955 when they decided to stay.

Eleven years later, I was born in Southampton, New York, the eighth of nine children. By the time I reached elementary school, my father was doing masonry work and my mom worked nights as a hospital union worker. I grew up literally across the railroad tracks in the working-class Black community of Bridgehampton, which along with similar small enclaves in Easthampton, Sag Harbor, and Southampton, made up what the local folk by the mid 1970s jokingly called "The Other Hampton." When I was eighteen, complications from an automobile accident years earlier claimed my father's life.

Before that, most of the details I remember about my father's parenting centered around the two main pillars of my childhood life outside of home: church and school. My parents had an obsession with matters of the soul. They were very much concerned that we not only knew the power of prayer, but also how to pray and how often. They wanted me to live as clean and respectful a Christian life as possible. They also expressed this through their church membership and attendance. There were many times when the family spent nearly as much time at church as at home. A deacon in the church, my father took great care for its maintenance. He was also superintendent of the Sunday school. On the surface, this was an oddity because my father only had a second-grade education. On closer inspection, given his obsession with education, it wasn't as inconsistent as it seemed.

Financial necessity ended my father's formal childhood schooling: his mom needed him to work to help support the household. So as an able-bodied seven-year-old he joined the other able bodies and began a work ethic my parents would pass on to me. Education was the only concern they had during my childhood that paralleled their focus on spiritual health. Education for my parents, like most of their generation, represented an end-all-be-all. My father was in his late forties when he attended night school and finally learned to read and earned his high school equivalency. In the meantime, any grades less than an "A" earned by his children were duly rewarded with an old school "spare not the rod"–level spanking. My father was the disciplinarian. I don't recall when it clicked for me that education was crucial, but I knew that without excellent grades, I'd have to face my father's wrath. As a child, being a student was my job. Therefore, I should work at it to the best of my ability, which in my parent's eyes meant being the best. There was no wavering on this.

The long-term result was that although neither of my parents finished high school, all of their children graduated college. But the idea of education as an end-all-be-all for most previous generations of African Americans was somehow still lost on my generation. We came of age with the deterioration of public education system, rising college costs, decline of living-wage jobs with benefits, the crack-cocaine explosion, a war on drugs, the escalation of incarceration from 200,000 in 1970 to over 2 million by the year 2000. It is no wonder that a recurring theme in hip-hop culture is that education is not a panacea: *The Miseducation of Lauryn Hill*, Kanye West's *College Dropout*, the many hip-hop artists who were high school dropouts—from Jay-Z, Nas, 50 Cent, and Eminem, who, like the Notorious B.I.G., worked this reality into their rhymes—

"considered a fool cause I dropped out of high school." In the midst of these upheavals, for us, education was reduced to a tool, at best.

If education—which had been a primary pillar of traditional Black American identity—was lost with the coming of the hip-hop era, then what has replaced it? As the 1970s turned to the early '80s, those of us who grew up hip-hop were caught up in the transition of the American Dream. Once defined as a good-paying job, modest home in the suburbs, and a comfortable middle-age life, the new American Dream was now millionaire status by twenty-five with all the trappings of extreme success: pricey cars, ostentatious mansions, exotic vacations, excessive jewelry, phat bank accounts, diversified investments, and more. Through it all, consumer culture tied to individual worth was its handmaiden. The emphasis that used to be placed on education had within our lifetime been shifted to the "get money" '80s, '90s and beyond. This transformation was a global capitalistic phenomenon that was defined nationally as Reaganomics. Its celluloid presentation came in the form of the '80s flicks *Wall Street*, *The Firm*, and later the hip-hop influenced *New Jack City*. Overnight, we have seemingly gone from a community who celebrated education and social uplift to one buried in stereotypes, where women are defiled and degraded, and money at all costs is our generation's end-all-be-all.

As the father of an eight-year-old son, what is the challenge of parenting a Black manchild in these times? I spend quality time with my son as much as possible, mostly on a daily basis. I call him from the road when I'm traveling and rarely spend weekends or more than three nights at a time away from home. We have dinner together most nights, routinely take walks and bike rides where we talk about current events, his day, my work, and his future. I am teaching him to talk to me so that when he needs me most, he will know that I am there.

I parent collectively with his mom in the tradition in which I learned from my parents. We immerse him in nurturing and safe environments—at home, school, and play—that reinforce a strong sense of his own value along with the value of others. We educate him at home and immerse him in the best schools we can afford. In this age of consumer culture, we are very concerned about media representations and are teaching him to be media literate. Rather than television, friends, video games, or extended child care, *we* intend to be his major influences. For us parenting includes taking responsibility for his development into a young man who is ready to make a meaningful contribution to the world.

"As the father of an eight-year-old son, what is the challenge of parenting a black manchild in these times?"

We take international trips with him as often as possible because we want him to see himself as larger than simply American, but a citizen of the world. It is the collaboration of our parent's generation's emphasis on education and our own generation's "get money" era philosophy (which influences our financial success) that have in part allowed us to do so.

On racial matters, I try to always strike a balance between a series of seeming opposites: We hip-hop generationers were raised at the tail end of the era where being Black generally meant you lived in a predominantly Black community. This is not my son's reality. His is a future where he must be cognizant of his relationship with and responsibility to other Black men. Finally, when it comes to race, my approach to parenting considers daily that our country is no longer exclusively Black and white and neither should his understanding of America's race dynamics be solely defined as such. Still, I must help my son to hold on to a sense of Black cultural identity and to respect the humanity of other cultures while understanding the white supremacist global culture that continues to adversely affect Black life.

When it comes to our generation's music, despite being one of hip-hop's most passionate defenders, I'm very selective about the hip-hop music that I expose my son to. This means the bulk of his music isn't hip-hop, or at best it's hip-hop classics. No strip-club-inspired music videos are part of his diet. This means, as dead prez reminds us, me "turn [ing] off the radio" and CDs that aren't age appropriate. I'm old-fashioned in the sense that I believe that there is entertainment for children, entertainment for adults, and entertainment that crosses the age divide. However, the adults in the room have to be adult enough to regulate that.

As I think about which lessons of my father's generation and my own to pass on to my son, more than anything my father said, I remember his deeds. So in my own parenting, I'm trying to pay more attention to the example I'm setting, the lifestyle I'm living, the company I keep, the causes I support. My hopes and prayers as a father are that my son will inherit a better world with better options; that he can live in a society that is respected for doing good rather than harm in the world; that he belongs to a generation that will use their education, their financial resources, and whatever new philoso-

phies they devise to move the nation and world to brighter days far removed from the madness of our time. My biggest challenge as a father is to do my part to help bring this world into existence.

*In my 2002 book *The Hip-Hop Generation: Young Blacks and the Crisis in African-American Culture*, I define the hip-hop generation as young Blacks born between 1965 and 1984. I maintain that usage throughout this essay. The generation born after this age group, those born between 1985 and 2004, often erroneously get lumped in with the hip-hop generation. However, these are two distinctive age groups—even if the younger age group identifies with hip-hop culture.

■

What Kind of Place is This?: A Black Father Raising His Sons in White Suburbia

▶ ALFORD A. YOUNG, JR.

My eight-year-old son has very few people his age to talk to about his favorite music. In the past two years, he has fallen in love with Hip-Hop. He first began listening to it while riding in the back-seat of the car, where the radio is usually locked in on the only Detroit-based urban contemporary radio station heard static-free in our hometown of Ann Arbor, Michigan. He now also watches Black Entertainment Television, as well as the cable television stations that play Hip-Hop music twenty-four hours a day. My son squeezes in these shows in the hour or so of television that he gets on weekday nights when school is in session. I am amused that he finds old-school Hip-Hop as appealing as the contemporary material. He has recently been trying to learn about the career of Big Daddy Kane, who hasn't had a hit record since my son was born. My little guy has also studied the role that James Brown has played in contributing to the birth of Hip-Hop—even discovering that James did not intentionally do so as much as have his music and style of performance respectfully appropriated by artists who were barely alive to witness the Godfather of Soul (even when he was past his prime). My wife and I have recently reached a point where we have to check in with our son to learn the names of some of the new artists and the records they have released. Yet, despite my son's serious investment in this music, he has very few friends to talk to about it.

I first began taking note of this situation two years ago, when Cassidy's "I'm a Hustler" came on the radio (of course, the edited version) as I was driving my son and his best friend to basketball practice one Tuesday. My son began to sing the chorus, and before he could get the second verse of "I'm a hustler, I'm a—I'm a hustler, homey" out of his mouth, his best friend said, in a matter-of-fact tone, "My parents don't let me listen to this record." Off went the radio. After all, I did not want to be the cause of any ill will with this boy's parents, two people I most respect in Ann Arbor. These two, and my wife and I, regularly discuss our sons' schooling and the tribulations of raising Black boys in a small, predominantly Caucasian city. One measure of satisfaction for us is that the boys are in the same classroom. Hence, at the time of this young man's remark I immediately settled on the idea that my son simply would have to sing that song out loud another day.

Over the past two years, I have discovered that many young Black men of my son's age in Ann Arbor are forbidden to listen to Hip-Hop. Like my son, these are boys in middle-class, white-collar professional families, with parents who are anxiously intent on seeing their children rise to—if not surpass—their own class standing. These parents are equally anxiety-ridden about the myriad threats and impediments that stand in the way of young Black men from achieving this end. While I understand the concerns that their parents have, I also realize that my motivation to allow both my sons to deviate from the Black middle-class norm and listen to Hip-Hop (my four-year-old now tries to sing along with his older brother) rests in the fact that, decades ago, my father freely allowed me to take in the rich culture of Black America as manifested in East Harlem, where I was born and raised.

When I was young, my dad helped me think about and make links between the 1960s, when Black American culture seemed to overwhelm American society in terms of music, dress, and language, and the 1980s, when it began to seem, to me, that urban-based African Americans were becoming the least valued people in the country. He exposed me to all of Harlem and the South Bronx, and in doing so allowed me to witness and make sense of that which was good and not so good about the qualities of life that people in these communities experienced. Although he was of white-collar, professional standing, he and my mother chose to live and raise my older sister and I in East Harlem, where the immense heroin distribution and consumption of the 1970s gave way to

the same dynamics with crack in the 1980s. At that time, Hip-Hop was the least threatening of social forces impinging upon my neighborhood. Yet, even if it could have been more problematic back then, I believe that my father would have had few qualms about allowing me to figure out what to embrace and what to reject about it. He

"Essentially, my wife and

I strug

[Al and his two boys]

le daily

to create spaces for our sons to make their own choices."

always supported me in making good choices about how to handle myself in the social environment that surrounded me.

Now, nearly two decades later, I think about my father's response to me while thinking about my own sons. In a physical sense, Ann Arbor is much safer than East Harlem. Culturally and psychologically, though, it often is a much riskier place to be a Black American boy. For example, my wife came home after visiting a preschool a few years ago to explain how thrilled the principal was that the school had enough Black boys in it so that every classroom could have one, thus denying these young men any meaningful interaction with each other during the formal school day. Hence, achieving diversity in this school meant denying the boys the chance to see and interact with each other in an academic setting. Examples like this abound in this town.

Accordingly, Black parents here must work especially hard at home with their sons (and daughters) to remedy this cultural malaise. In my home, the work to do so involves open sharing with my oldest son stories of slavery and oppression, as well as resilience and commitment to struggle. I often do so through the large video library that I maintain, where my oldest and I watch material on African-American history. We openly discuss the violence visited upon Black Americans, and the threats that still remain in being a Black man in America. Furthermore, I generally follow the principle that anything my sons ask about is fair terrain for conversation, even if the conversations might end with my explaining that some things we can talk about at home, but not in public spaces. This is why I have little anxiety about exposing my children to Hip-Hop music when many other African American parents in my community care not to do so.

Essentially, my wife and I struggle daily to create spaces for our sons to make their own choices. In doing so, a part of the struggle is reconciling with the fact that neither she nor I believe that Hip-

Hop music is the threatening phenomenon that many people make it out to be (after all, given our early life experiences in New York City, we think we have a pretty good idea about what can really be threatening). We simply encourage the boys to understand and think seriously about the language in some of that music, and the images associated with it, and to not valorize that which is so heavily proliferated about that music in mainstream venues. She and I have seen that it is far too easy to misread a lot about Black cultural expression when you are a young Black male in a place like Ann Arbor. We also talk to each other about the contrasts in some of our approaches and those taken by the parents of many of my sons' friends. Ultimately, we hope that our approach will result in the development of two Black men who value their Blackness, who understand how threatening that Blackness is to many other Americans, and who have the self-love and understanding to navigate their lives so that they can become all that they can in life without fear or hesitancy.

In many ways, this is all bottled up in the way in which I talked to my oldest son a few hours after basketball practice that Tuesday. I talked about why his best friend is not allowed to listen to "I'm a Hustler" and how, even though he is allowed to do so, he should think about the lyrics in that song, and the actual life experience of Cassidy (who served time for involuntary manslaughter), and understand that the complexities of life as a Black American means that he has to maintain a critical perspective of all that he is exposed to even while his parents aggressively strive to promote that exposure.

■

A Moment of Clarity

▶ AARON LLOYD

The multitude of complex issues surrounding fatherhood has always been a contentious topic in the modern Black family. In the last thirty years, however, there has been a consistent, yet oft-ignored voice weighing in on the issue, and it is not the linchpin of the Black community, the Black church; that voice is the hip-hop community, and one would need only a cursory glance to verify its long history of commentary on fatherhood. LL Cool J, for example, weighed in rather late in his career on the track "Father"—the autobiographical tale of his father's shooting of his mother and grandfather. Also, Jay-Z has mentioned his fatherly woes throughout his entire career—on the honest and personal account "Moment of Clarity;" the cautionary fictional tale "Meet the Parents;" and on the Beanie Sigel–assisted, pain-driven plea "Where Have You Been?" Even cultural icon Tupac Shakur weighed in on the topic during his pre–Death Row days on his heartfelt "Papaz's Song." Notably, when these and other rappers address fatherhood they all do so from a shared viewpoint, that of having an absentee father. Hip-hop culture has made it clear, in many ways, that the absent father is a potent unresolved issue in our community.

That same issue is also my life story. Like countless others, I was born into an impoverished Black neighborhood. My mother and father were no different from their peers. They were young, dumb, and full of . . . love. Sixteen when they met, their union led to my birth and their marriage—in that exact order. I was born in August and attended their wedding later that year in December. By the time I turned three, however, my mother and father were living in different domiciles, had birthed my sister, and were separated permanently. After they separated, my father was gone from my life for about a decade.

I was a teenager when I saw my father again. In essence, I was meeting him for the very first time and, as a result, we had relationship issues right out the gate. I was four feet nothing, timid, and as shy as a boy could possibly be. In contrast, my father was six-feet-four, two hundred ten pounds, confident, and as manly as one would want a male to be. In addition to dealing with the intimidating physical differences, I had to deal with emotional intimidations, too. This "nameless" man showed up on my porch one day expecting immediate and unearned respect. How do I address such a man, my father no less, who I had never met before? I could not find it in me to call him Dad. That was too personal. Still, I cringed when I addressed him by his first name, Hank. So, I came up with a solution that only an emotionally retarded teenager could possibly think was a good idea: I would mumble or speak softly whenever I addressed him. In other instances, I would just use sentences that avoided calling him by name. I pulled off this game for entire weekend visits until I could finally bring myself to call him Dad.

Things stayed frayed between us throughout my teen and young adult years. My father had several opportunities to be a responsible father, but he often came up short. He agreed to get dental braces for me but only paid for the initial part of the work. Without his promised support, I was forced to take them off. When I decided to go to college, he committed to pay my tuition, but then reneged one week prior to the start of classes. I ended up working in a Friendly's Ice Cream parlor earning minimum wage instead of maximizing my education as planned. On another occasion, my father threatened to skip my wedding because of monetary issues. He eventually came to his senses and attended anyway. These and other situations were all opportunities for my father to step up to the plate, yet each time he only ended up hurting me worse than before. His arrogance did not allow him to acknowledge his shortcom-

ings or the fact that he abandoned my sister and me. A sincere admission of guilt and evidence of actual repentance is all anyone really wants when wronged by loved ones. One would think I would have learned not to expect or desire much from him as I was growing up, but a child will always love their parent—from the tips of their fingers to the recesses of their soul. They will always want the nurturing of their parents, even if history proves this a foolish desire.

My father and I endured our own personal cold war until a day came that caused a major change in our lives. It was a normal day, extraordinary in no particular way. He was at my house visiting when he mentioned, in passing, an upcoming colon exam that he'd scheduled with his doctor. Ironically, I had just started a new job related to the health field and had become a sudden expert on the human colon. I knew to suggest a more thorough examination. He took my advice and scheduled a more complete exam. Several months later, my father announced that he had colon cancer. I was caught totally off guard. Cancer. Colon cancer? My dad had always been the picture of health to me. Invincible. In almost the same breath, my father revealed that he had already gone through his cancer diagnosis, treatment, chemotherapy, *and* had already beaten the disease.

He had kept his physical and emotional pain a secret from the family all this time. The treatment was over, he had survived, and I had experienced his diagnosis, treatment, and recovery in less than three minutes.

My father's health was fine, but he was a different man in so many ways. Beside his serious weight loss and severely darkened fingernails from the chemotherapy (which shamefully, I failed to notice initially), he was different in a nonphysical way also. Apparently, facing his own mortality made Hank take stock of his life. It forced him to come to talk to me about more than just his health. All the anger I had toward him was brought to the surface as I listened to him earnestly apologize for a laundry list of wrongs. In particular, he said he was sorry for the emotional and financial hardships that my sister, my mother, and I endured because of his absenteeism. Cold war over! I eagerly relented, forgave, hugged, and cried with my father as if we were shooting the movie of the week for the Hallmark Channel. I was shocked further by the aftermath of this breakthrough. I had not realized that I was carrying around an emotional bag of bricks. When I forgave my dad and put it down it was like breathing fresh air.

My relationship with my father continues to grow in positive increments and is now one of the daily joys of my adulthood. I am more comfortable with him and still seek his nurturing guidance. The truest example of that was when I was suffering from a grave illness. I was hospitalized in an intensive care unit and completely unaware of my surroundings. At bedside were my doctors, friends, and family members but I was totally unable to identify any of

▸ [Aaron as a little boy and his father: goin' fishing; Aaron and Hank: at Aaron's wedding: more good times]

them—except my father. In my delirium, I, on some deep level, was able to respond to my father only. Throughout my haze and suffering, our bond endured—remaining strong. Father and son in a moment of clarity.

Though my dad and I have both survived life-threatening health crises, my fatherhood story is not a fairy tale. There is no perfect ending. We still have conflicts. That's the nature of the beast called life. What is different, however, is how we approach our conflicts. We don't let our issues hold the significance today that they once did. We keep them in proper prospective. Our reconciliation allowed me to revisit old issues, but from a fresh perspective, minus the overt anger, victimization, and general "woe is me" attitude that was buried inside of me.

The definitive song on fatherhood was made by rapper Ed O.G. and Da Bulldogs with his 1991 self-explanatory classic "Be a Father to Your Child." The powerful women in my life—those who loved, raised, and protected me—did everything for me except prepare me for manhood, for that is something that only a man can teach a boy.

Jazz, Hip-Hop, and Dad In My Subconscious

▶ SHAUN NEBLETT

Before I started praying and expressing gratitude, music is what blocked negative emotions from infiltrating my subconscious. I was in grade school during the 1980s when my father suggested positive things to me—subconsciously. For example, he used to brag about how quickly I could put Hot Wheels race car tracks together, suggesting that I was smart and that he was proud of me. I thought that was awesome. But more than anything, I loved that he thought I was special and that he thought we were friends.

I remember that my dad, who was born in Panama, used to cook. He made goats, pigs, and chicken gizzards—palatable dinners for me and my older brother. I also remember the West Indian Black Power radio station was always on when he drove me to school in his AT&T company van. Even though I would slouch so no one could see me, I was comfortable because I was in my dad's care. One time he stopped the van in front of a Catholic church in downtown Orange, New Jersey and told me to look up. I couldn't see anything at first. Then he pointed my eyes in the right direction. All the way at the top of the building, I saw a shiny gold Jesus with outstretched hands, blessing whatever was below. Neither my dad nor I have ever been big on church, but I felt a breathtaking feeling pass between the two of us that sunny morning. Those van rides were another constant suggestion that my dad and I shared an inseparable bond. He even used to show me that I could blow a booger out my nose if I covered one nostril up and blew real hard in spurts.

My father never called himself an alcoholic, but he drank a lot. I

began realizing that he was a drinker during my middle school years. When my father drank liquor his actions were no longer positive or awesome. His actions caused me to foster subliminal thoughts that something was wrong with me. The nights he drank he hardly said a word to me. Instead, he'd drink and have phone conversations with a woman who wasn't my mom. Some Saturday nights, he'd have a drink or two and then take off, leaving us at home in Jersey while he spent the night in Brooklyn. My dad and I were once friends, but now his drinking led to actions that suggested he didn't even want to be associated with my mother, brother, or me. We didn't even seem to matter.

One of my first subconscious responses to my father's drinking was giving up on hip-hop. I was in the seventh or eighth grade, one night, in my room flicking through channels. Dude had just gone to the bathroom down the hallway (staying on the toilet for thirty or forty minutes had become one of his customs when he drank). I changed the channel to a rap video and it must have been on for only twenty seconds when I heard the toilet flush and the bathroom door burst open. Dad was in such a rush to get to my bedroom that he was still trying to fix his pants when he appeared. Stunned, he did a double take at the TV, and then at me . . . back at the TV and then to me again. Then he said, with the greatest sense of pride even though he wasn't sober, "Oh!!!! You listen to rap music now!!!"

That night I feared my dad didn't like me. He knew that I liked jazz music. He knew I was learning to play the saxophone. He even bragged to people about how I would play his Cannonball Adderley record over and over again. Why was he now so excited that I was listening to hip-hop?, or so he thought. Was he saying that I needed to toughen up? Did he think I wasn't cool because I loved jazz music? Back then, only the tough West Indian kids on my block were listening to rap. I had heard my father say that the sons of his people out in Brooklyn were into that hip-hop stuff, as though that was cool. But when my father was sober, he never mentioned rap music. Plus, the West Indian Black Power radio station that he always played denounced the music almost every day on the ride home in that van. So the suggestion that was made—that night my father stumbled into my bedroom in the middle of his drunken routine—was that I was now somehow cool because I was watching a rap video instead of listening to jazz. That suggestion spread through my subconscious, and from that moment on I didn't want anything to do with hip-hop. After

"That night I feared my dad didn't like me."

that night, I associated it as something that I was not cool enough to be a part of. I would shy away from conversations about rappers, albums dropping, or new videos. I didn't realize that I was missing out on some of the greatest cultural activity of African-American history. I was too tied up thinking that the music was a symbol of tough guys whose image I doubted I could fit in with. I was convinced that my father felt that way too.

As more episodes occurred throughout high school, jazz music protected me from totally giving up on my father. I remember, prior to my adolescence, he would say, "Shaun always impressed me because if there was one record he did like since he was young, it was *Mercy, Mercy, Mercy* by Cannonball." My dad's suggestion that listening to jazz was a talent that I was blessed with had a long-lasting effect. By the time I began college, I had more jazz artists in my CD collection than he had in his entire eclectic record collection. I would stay in my room and listen to John Coltrane, Charlie Mingus, Miles, Yusef Lateef, and others while my Dad sat in the living room or kitchen savoring a drink. Although I had stopped talking to him (something inside of me wouldn't even allow me to look him in the eye when we *had* to say something to each other), I believe that jazz music was a subconscious way of holding on to something I had picked up from this man.

I was in my early twenties when hip-hop manifested itself in my life again. My homeboy Salahadeen was driving me home from work one day. We made a stop on 125th Street so he could pay a bill. He got out of the car, but kept the music on while I waited. An Isaac Hayes song started to play, and then Jay-Z started talking over the music—about hustling being an action of desperation. Then the tempo sped up and in between yelling "Can I Live?," Jay was rapping about persevering through life no matter what problems lingered. What he was rapping must have taken the form of solid matter as it rippled through the air because I felt Jay-Z's words hitting me. I felt the song reprogramming me. By the time Salahadeen returned, I realized that hip-hop was something I could associate with and that I had to let go of conceptions I had subconsciously formed during middle school.

I started listening to hip-hop on the regular. Because I stepped into the arena so late, I had the luck of listening to rappers from the beginning of their careers to points in their careers when they started changing their craft. If the change was for the worse I would move on and see what suggestions another rapper had to offer. I was impacted by Jay-Z and Nas the most. I felt Jay-Z when he said, "I'm bravin' temperatures below zero / no hero / no father figure / you gotta pardon a *n-word*." I appreciated Nas's father playing trumpet on his son's tracks. On "Bridging the Gap" Olu Dara spoke of his son and said, "I named the boy Nasir, all the boys call him Nas / I told him as a youngster, he'll be the greatest man alive."

But Jay-Z and Nas weren't responsible for me reconciling issues with my father. I had learned that prayer and being grateful were means of feeding my subconscious. It's when I started to regularly give thanks for my father that I suggested to myself that my Dad is of great worth to me. I took notice of the invaluable ways that he influenced me. As I started to pray for him to improve his lifestyle, the years of anger subsided. I gained faith that my dad still loves me. I learned that when Black men begin to free our minds of the fears, worries, and doubts that were caused by deeply distressing or disturbing experiences with our fathers, then something inside will guide us to live the lives that we dream of having.

■

"AND THERE IS THE DEEP LONGING FOR THE BREAD OF LOVE

 EVERYBODY WISHES TO LOVE AND BE LOVED.

 HE WHO FEELS THAT HE IS NOT LOVED FEELS THAT

 HE DOES NOT COUNT."

—1963 SERMON BY DR. MARTIN LUTHER KING, JR.

"A KNOCK AT MIDNIGHT"

The "Pursuit" of Meaning

▸ BILL STEPHNEY

Seemingly concurrent with the annual January 15th celebration of the birthday of Dr. Martin Luther King, Jr., the dependable suppositions come forth from the usual suspects: "Ya' know, if Dr. King were alive today and turned on the radio or TV, he'd get depressed," or "Ya' know, if Dr. King were alive today, he'd change his speech to 'I Have A Nightmare' . . ." There might be some truth to those assumptions. Between the combination of actual press coverage, statistical analysis, and the unrelenting portrayal of criminal/street "realism" by the current Hip Hop media industry, the status for an unreasonable portion of African Americans, especially young males, only rivals the ozone layer for predictions of impending extinction.

As it exists, the picture for many of these young men is bleak: homicide rates in a number of the nation's major cities, are steadily driving back to 1980s crack-trade levels. High-profile police

shootings, like that of the late Sean Bell, the high school pitching phenom from Queens, New York, slain hours before his wedding, dominate local TV news updates. The universe of professional sports, once sheltered from the sort of sudden violence that has claimed some of rap's biggest names, finds itself eulogizing for NFL cornerback Darrent Williams, lost to a drive-by on his limousine. Yet in the midst of all the pain comes the possibility. Emerging from this troubled climate—Dr. King would be given to analogizing it to the "biblical Egypt"—is a fairly organic "wave" (I would stop short of characterizing it as a "movement") of discussions, organizations, recordings, and movies trumpeting the importance of fatherhood in the African-American community. As it is believed, a generation of men is vowing that their children will not face the same hardships and uncertainty of life that they faced. And a rapper shall lead them.

Will Smith, once known on boom boxes and turntables as "The Fresh Prince" (along with his dexterous spinning partner DJ Jazzy Jeff), and later as a network sitcom and screen star, had the surprise movie smash of the moment with *The Pursuit Of Happyness*. In *Pursuit*, Smith morphs into the real-life story of Chris Gardner, a successful African-American investment broker, who in his bootstrap beginnings, struggled to support his wife and young son during the early 1980s. The struggle overwhelms the Gardner family structure, and when his wife leaves him he instantly becomes a single father with a young son. Gardner's personal, yet heroic reality series follows the requisite Hollywood narrative patterns, as his loving commitment to his son drives him to overcome homelessness and despair. (The stroke of production genius was the casting choice of putting Will and actress Jada Pinkett-Smith's actual son Jaden in the film—the natural, nurturing eye contact between the father and son essentially became reality portraying reality). No sane student of box-office receipts would ever question Smith's bankability; his films have had an average gross of approximately $160 million; *Pursuit*, however, was expected to be a "small" film for him. Clearly "size" did matter here, as *Pursuit* opened at number one in its first week, making an estimated $26.5 million. After three weeks, the film approached $130 million.

What may be in play for *Pursuit* is the Holy Grail of circumstance for us entertainment types: zeitgeist. Though recently released statistics evidence a still-climbing national out-of-wedlock birthrate (with the African-American rate flatlining at its constantly unacceptable 69 percent level), the push for Black father commitment, marriage or not, continues forward. In February of 2007, Lions Gate Entertainment partnered with the one-man gospel media industrial complex known as Tyler Perry to release Perry's then new effort, *Daddy's Little*

Girls. In it, Iris Elba (of my personal television obsession, HBO's *The Wire*) plays a single father trying to raise three daughters on an auto mechanic's wage. All of this while living in the "might-be-gentrified-one-day-but-not-right-now" section of Atlanta.

African-American fatherhood conferences, publications, Web sites, and low-income fatherhood initiatives are sprouting up all over. There are veterans, like Baltimore's The Center for Fathers, Families and Workforce Development, run by Joe Jones. Also, there are smaller efforts, like one headed by twenty-something Anwan Wesley of Pittsburgh, who, after surviving a near-fatal stabbing and the killing of a best friend, has gone on to become a doting daddy of two boys and publisher of *Fatherhood Magazine*. Added to the mix: nearly every rap CD features a track touching on father/family matters. Juelz Santana, for example, of the rapper collective called The Dipset, told popular website AllHipHop.com in 2005 about his song "Daddy": "I feel like every man needs that father figure in their life, so I just wanted to express that in that song—so my son can always go back and listen to it whether I'm here, God bless, or not here, when he's old enough to really hear what I'm talkin' 'bout."

In the Hip Hop generation (in urban communities, I estimate the age demographic to be between twenty-five to forty years old), the once common notions of love, marriage, commitment, devotion, and fatherhood have become abstract concepts. Ironically, among the 1980s and '90s babies, a number of us who've been practitioners of the Hip Hop "aesthetic" have focused on the issues of family through lyrics, music videos, poetry, and as we've recently seen, film. While urban family policy has tended to be a third rail for legislators and activists, dating back to the Civil Rights generation's outrage over the 1965 Department of Labor report titled: *The Negro*

Family: A Case For National Action, Hip Hop's penchant for ugly honesty has allowed it to rip the scab off a painful issue.

Some have observed that the first battleground for Black fathers challenging their marginalization was the Memphis Garbage Workers Strike of 1968, in which Dr. King was a leader (and later, a brutal casualty). Taylor Rogers, one of the striking laborers, said during an interview from the revelatory 1990 PBS documentary *Eyes On The Prize II*: "I had seven kids in school . . . trying to educate my kids, trying to buy a home. It was really rough, but I knew something had to happen. We couldn't continue on making $1.04 an hour." When Hip Hop culture began its development in the 1970s fiscal-crisis-ravaged Bronx and Manhattan, the national rate of Black nonmarital childbearing had risen to approximately 50 percent of children born that year. In addition, largely due to changing sexual mores and values, the divorce rate for all U.S. couples skyrocketed. By 1994, an astounding 70 percent of all Black children were born out of wedlock. By this point, the idea that Black children were intended to be raised mostly by biological mothers and fathers in the same household had all but evaporated. Moreover, the notion that fathers/men were equally as important to their families as mothers/women had largely been rejected culturally and through social policy. Years of near advocacy that Black men were "optional" in the raising and nurturing of children took an effect.

> **"It was really rough, but I knew something had to happen."**

Today, much of the anger expressed in Rap and Hip Hop represents a cry out against that Black male marginalization. In these "hoods," some young men are looking for meaning—in surroundings where their futures are not so apparent. Others, however, yet to develop a sense of their own humanity, join gang/thug life to achieve the adult male guidance they miss within their household and neighborhoods. They become, to use the unfortunate term heard even in R&B top-charting songs, "soldiers" lost in the fog of war on the streets. Columbia University professor Ronald B. Mincy, an academic pioneer in the study of African-American males and family policy, told the *New York Times* in 2006: "Over the last two decades, the economy did great," Mr. Mincy said, "and low-skilled women, helped by public policy, latched onto it . . . we spent $50 billion in efforts that produced the turnaround for poor women. We are not even beginning to think about the men's problem on similar orders of magnitude."

Perhaps those of us within media and entertainment, understanding the futility of waiting for bureaucracies to address conditions that they exacerbated in the first place, are employing our own skill sets to change the climate. I don't think it would be clichéd to point out today, that in the most significant speech given by a most significant thinker and organizer, Dr. King did intone that all citizens would be "guaranteed the unalienable rights of life, liberty and the pursuit of happiness." Hmm . . . the end of that phrase sounds like a good title for an optimistic book and a movie. Let's see if we can get a rapper to star in it.

■

▶ [Talib, his mother Brenda Greene, his children Diana and Amani Greene, and his brother Jamal Greene]

An Interview with Talib Kweli

I FIRST MET TALIB KWELI IN 2002 THROUGH WORK I WAS DOING WITH HIS MOTHER, DR. BRENDA GREENE. SHE AND I HAD BEEN WORKING ON A FEW LITERARY ARTS PROJECTS AT MEDGAR EVERS COLLEGE AND THAT LED HER TO ASK ME TO CONSIDER AN INTERIM EXECUTIVE DIRECTOR POSITION AT THE NKIRU CENTER FOR EDUCATION AND CULTURE. NKIRU WAS A NONPROFIT LITERARY ARTS ORGANIZATION AND BOOKSTORE THAT TALIB AND DANTE "MOS DEF" SMITH HAD ACQUIRED IN BROOKLYN, AND OF WHICH SHE WAS THE CHAIR (TALIB'S FATHER, DR. PERRY GREENE, WAS ALSO ON THE BOARD, AS WERE DANTE'S PARENTS). I ACCEPTED THE POSITION. WHAT WAS SUPPOSED TO BE A FOUR-MONTH QUICK HIT TURNED INTO A YEAR LONG JOURNEY.

IT WAS DURING THAT TIME THAT I GOT A CLOSER PEEK AT TALIB AND EXPERIENCED FIRSTHAND HIS CONSISTENT FOCUS ON HELPING PEOPLE AND HIS LONGING FOR THE BLACK COMMUNITY TO ELEVATE ITSELF. MANY HIGH-PROFILE ARTISTS DON'T HAVE THOUGHTS ABOUT HOW THEIR TIME, TALENT, AND TREASURE CAN BE USED TOWARD THE IMPROVEMENT OF THEIR COMMUNITIES. TALIB IS AN EXCEPTION. AS A MAN, HE IS HIGHLY PERCEPTIVE, OUTSPOKEN, CRITICAL, AND CONFIDENT OF HIS ROLE IN THE WORLD, AND IN ALL THINGS, HE IS LOVING. AS AN ARTIST, HE IS ONE OF THE MOST TALENTED THAT THIS GENERATION HAS EVER SEEN AND HIP-HOP IS BETTER BECAUSE OF HIS GIFTS. WHAT FOLLOWS IS A GLIMPSE OF THESE ATTRIBUTES, WRAPPED UP IN A QUICK CHAT ABOUT FATHERHOOD.

ARS: What are your overall feelings about fatherhood, and then fatherhood as it relates to African-American men?

Talib: Fatherhood is the realization that the world no longer revolves around you. It is the understanding that the best you have to offer has yet to come. Fatherhood for Africans in America means teaching your children how to live when survival is the real challenge. Hip hop music has provided this generation with a code that allows us to begin correcting some of the mistakes of our predecessors. The hip hop music I speak of is not the mindless drivel on the airwaves, but the music that speaks to the soul of real people in the community.

My personal experience tells me that the statistics lie about how black fathers participate in the lives of their children. The courts were not involved in our families back in the day to the same extent they are now and men were allowed to run rampant and destroy their families. However, it was behind closed doors (and women who divorced were scorned). We have developed a court system that tries to remedy some of this, but we have also created a situation where good men are treated like deadbeats because of the sins of our fathers. Many of the young black men I know who grew up without fathers try their hardest to reverse the pattern, not continue it.

ARS: Given all that, what key things do you think Black men must do, those who came of age with hip hop, to create or continue healthy relationships with their sons and daughters?

Talib: (1) We have to stop depending on the courts to decide what is right for our families. We must put the welfare of our children above our personal gain; (2) We must embrace our own history and culture; (3) We can never let being proud to be black, be corny [and] we have to stop depending on music, TV, even schools, to raise our children. [That] starts in the home, especially [during this] information age; and, (4) We must redefine the idea of family, and see community as family. If it ever took a village, it takes one now.

ARS: Some argue that hip hop culture was the replacement "father figure" in many Black men's lives . . . filling in the role for absentee dads. Would you agree?

Talib: One of my best friends told me that he didn't know his father, so his morals and values were learned from hip hop records. That was direct first-person testimony and it is very true. Hip hop is male dominated and teaches you how to *appear* like a man.

ARS: Your life on the road as a hip hop recording artist is different than the lives of most Black men, and it's certainly different than the life that your parents lead. What are the key differences between how you were raised and how you are raising your children?

Talib: The way that I deal with money and the amount of information I share with my children is drastically different than how my parents raised me. As teachers, they were forced to stick to a budget to get by. As a touring musician, my income fluctuates so money is more of a means to an end than something to be saved. I have to find new ways to get my children to be frugal, because as an adult I've developed a lifestyle where the amount of work I put in directly affects how much I can make. Also, information comes at my children quicker and in bigger chunks, so I have to be quick on my feet.

ARS: What lessons did you learn from your father that you are now sharing with your two children?

Talib: Education is the key of a wonderful life. Never accept anything for what it is, always look beneath the surface. Treat everyone with the same compassion and caring you would like to receive. Work hard, harder than those around you.

■

[SIDE B]

My Son's Imaginary Friend

▸ JAMES BRAXTON PETERSON II

My son has an imaginary friend named Braxton. Braxton goes by the middle name I share with my son. It is my grandfather's name; he was James Braxton Peterson, the first, if you will. Known to his grandchildren as Pop-Pop.

My son's imaginary friend emerges from a lineage of strong men who worked hard to keep their families intact. For three generations, the Peterson men have embodied strength and perseverance; and more than he can imagine, my eight-year-old son has already started on the journey of continuing our legacy.

This legacy started with Pop-Pop's father, who was born a slave. His grizzled eighty-year-plus grille contained the pain of our ancestors. His permanent facial expression grimly enshrined our history in its corrugated folds. I can remember feeling his pride as we watched Hank Aaron smash what's-his-name's home-run record. Pop-Pop didn't say a word, but his steely emotions always emanated from him. As legend would have it, Braxton (the man who inspired our names) was a well-known rabble rouser in the early 1830s, near Jerusalem, Virginia—Nat Turner's stomping grounds. Braxton was considered one of the meanest, most rambunctious dudes alive. Some of that spirit runs through all three of us James Braxton Petersons.

Pop-Pop bore the brunt of that meanness

and muffled it up amongst all of the hatred and racism that he no doubt endured throughout his life. He was a rock of a family man: a sanitation worker and a working-class homeowner who kept his cars in exquisite condition. His anger and frustration at life and at the challenges of being a Black man in the early 1900s were channeled into his character, his work ethic, and his commitment to family. In addition to our name, Pop-Pop's strong character, work ethic, and commitment to family are tools that he passed on to me and my son. The harnessed power of Braxton's fiery figure, manifest.

My son Lil James (LJ) was born on my twenty-eighth birthday at 8:14 AM. I didn't even know it was my birthday when he was born. My wife had serious challenges during LJ's gestation, but I had put my wager on my seed at his conception. My confidence in his (be)coming and in his mother's health were unshakable. James Braxton Peterson, III's arrival cemented the nucleus of our family. His birthday, coinciding with and simultaneously superceding mine, is a miracle that I am still trying to grasp. The spiritual, cosmological, and astrological alignment blows me away everyday. He is my planned unplanned baby boy.

Now enter Braxton, LJ's imaginary friend. Braxton arrived on the scene around the time that LJ learned we were moving from Drexel Hill (just outside of Philadelphia) to Lewisburg (just outside of the middle of nowhere—central Pennsylvania). I had never really thought of imaginary childhood friends as a "Black" thing until I read the plight of Pecola in Toni Morrison's classic *The Bluest Eye*. Pecola used her imagination to wrestle with self-hatred, sexual assault, and rape. This forced me to think about how these imaginary friends come to be. Nonetheless, I was still surprised by the birth of imaginary Braxton.

As a self-professed doting father, over both my son and my daughter, I (and my wife, as well), had been worried over the move from Philly. Both of our children were born in Philadelphia and each lived in west and/or southwest Philadelphia for the first two to four years of their lives. City living can be good for children, but both my children now appreciate being able to play outside, preferring grass to concrete most days. A change of environment is a powerful educational tool for raising children. LJ loves our old neighborhoods, but having traveled to various places throughout this country at such a young age has given him enough geographic experience to be very selective about where he lives and where he plays.

Braxton has the coolness of Hip Hop running through his imaginary veins. He handled our transition from Philly to central Pennslvania with ease. Judging from the conversations between my children and Braxton, his presence helped them to settle in by offering them comfort in a new and initially strange land. Braxton is always part of the crew and their mission was always to build camaraderie and consensus for LJ in the absence of missed friends and family in Philadelphia. Braxton usually emerges when my son and/or daughter need an opinion or support for a cause. Or sometimes he's there just to say something that LJ may not feel comfortable saying himself. I love that LJ's mind works this way even though the fact that he had to rely on Braxton was, for me, somewhat upsetting. Only through the process of writing this have I come to realize how significant it is that the name of my son's imaginary friend is Braxton. Some aspects of Braxton are clearly products of my son's own personality—for instance, Braxton loves video games—and some aspects of Braxton were also clearly me— he loves Hip Hop.

One of the most important challenges for a father in the twenty-first century is to directly engage the culture of his children. Authentic knowledge of youth culture helps us to teach our children how to critically engage all forms of media and technology. This is a parental mandate for the globalized digital climate of our times. I have to be able to read with my son, play ball with him, coach him, play video games with him, use the computer with him, pray with him, listen to music with him, and converse with Braxton with him. Being a part of and a presence in all of his activities early on is crucial now because some of this access and influence is fleeting in fatherhood; especially as children become teens and the influence of technology on their lives expands infinitely. Some of these technological tools enhance a father's capacity to raise his children. Yet no technology—be it cell phone, iPod, video game, or e-mail—can displace a child's need for a father or fatherly figures.

I used to experience a twinge of awkward guilt when playing with my son amongst friends of his who do not have fathers involved in their lives. I felt like an imaginary father to them in those fleeting moments. This twinge of guilt eventually gave way to my understanding of the central challenge of capable Hip Hop generation fathers: we must function as fathers within our communities in addition to fulfilling this role in our families. The surest way to counter the conspiracies to destroy Black boys is for each able father to extend his paternal reach beyond his own nuclear family. This can be accomplished in an astonishing variety of ways—through church, Big Brothers / Big Sisters, the classroom, and the corners. Any way we do it, it must be done. There is a well-known, well-documented, and overemphasized father shortage in our communities. Which able-bodied fathers will step up to meet this challenge? Parenting our disadvantaged youth is the only strategy that ensures the future of our communities.

This parenting must, by necessity, take on various forms. The most important or primary form is the most direct—be a father to your own child/ren. I hope that this goes without saying. TAKE CARE OF YOURS! The second form is doing fatherly work that extends beyond the boundaries of our nuclear families. We need to actively input fatherly guidance and energy into our mosques, churches, schools, and the streets. The third form is that fathering which derives itself from our historical imagination. The ways in which we imagine our histories as fathers and sons through storytelling, literature, film, and music will no doubt aid us in this transition from fatherless to fathered. This is how Braxton helps LJ navigate the challenges of his own particular transition from Philly to Lewisburg, Pennsylvania. My son's imaginary friend emerges out of his own history—a history that provides comfort and support, consensus, and camaraderie in times of need. I can now proudly take note that my son's imaginary friend is named after me and after his great-grandfather. He imagines his support beyond our nuclear family into the history that undergirds our relationship: father to son, but also and at the same time, grandfather to grandson, great-grandfather to great-grandson, and so on.

■

"TAKE

CARE

OF YOURS!"

The Black Hair Matrix: How Jada Pinkett-Smith Saved My Daughter's Self-Esteem

▸ ADISA BANJOKO

Since 1987, I have been observing, writing, and speaking about Hip-Hop culture and its worldwide impact. I have been happily married to a beautiful Black woman for twelve years and I am a proud father of two (one boy/one girl). My daughter (we call her Baby Girl) is quite beautiful, despite my influence on her looks. Since her birth, I have described myself as a "recovering sexist." My daughter's existence has opened my eyes to many things I never cared about. For this and many other reasons, I thank Allah for her everyday.

Like most fathers, I want my daughter to be a physically, mentally, and spiritually secure woman. However, I know that America works hard to break the psyche of the Black woman—on countless levels. From skin lighteners to hair strengtheners, there has always been a psychological attack on the Black woman's mindset. Unfortunately, in recent times, Hip-hop music has come to play a proactive role in the attempted destruction of her self-esteem. It took me a long time to notice that by openly or quietly championing the music, videos, books, magazines, and movies that attack her essence, I was part of the problem. Being a father now, I cannot help but feel guilt akin to being the getaway driver in the car that jacked the Black woman's soul.

The initial attack begins with the indoctrination of what is considered beautiful. The American media machine has driven Black women to question their own beauty before they are even aware of what is happening. This assault in reality affects all non-White females (any female who lacks the traditional Anglo features). Not only do they question what beauty is, they question its very existence in their lives.

My daughter, like many American girls, is beaten over the head with Disney propaganda (and other kid networks) that predominately shows white women as royalty. From Cinderella to Ariel, she is bombarded with the notion that female leaders have pale skin and long flowing blond hair. Black female queens, leaders, and "beautiful" princesses make up less than one percent of children's cartoons/movies. Before you ask, no, Brandy does not count. They never use her in the Disney pantheon of princess brides: using her briefly as Cinderella does not wash away the years of neglect. Why is it Disney has never been able to show a beautiful young African princess?

Anyway, we normally have Baby Girl rockin' Afro puffs (thanks to the rapper Lady of Rage), or some braid pattern. I had never thought about how much self-esteem Lady of Rage's "Afro Puffs" track gave to many young Black women. Even though the song itself is not about hair—the hook, "I rock rough and stuff with my Afro puffs" makes Black women smile a little wider when they hear it. I actually spoke to Rage one day and thanked her for making that song. She told me that she took that style from a photo she saw of her aunt from the '70s. It is funny how one photo or one song can change so much. But I never really thought about the politics of Black women's hair—until the other day.

One morning about two years ago, my wife spent the morning hours styling Baby Girl's hair to resemble the look worn by Jada

"The American media machine has driven Black women

Pinkett-Smith (as the character Niobi) in *The Matrix Reloaded*. As we went about our day, people would comment on how beautiful Baby Girl looked, on how amazing her hairstyle made her shine. We still have wonderful photos of her from the first time she rocked that hairstyle. But this was *before* my daughter had been affected by the Black Hair Matrix, the thought of long flowing hair, and the ideal of European beauty.

About three months ago, my wife did Baby Girl's hair in the same fashion she had done two years before. She looked just as adorable as she did then—that Niobi hairstyle really looks great on her. Of course, Baby Girl was not able to see her hairstyle until her mother completed the styling. My wife was very excited for Baby Girl to look at herself in the mirror to see and understand how adorable she is. Once her style was completed, Baby Girl jumped up and raced back to the full-length mirror in her brother's bedroom. To everyone's surprise, she came out crying. Baby Girl was devastated. She told her mother that her hair was ugly. Baby Girl acted as if my wife was trying to humiliate her by not giving her hair like the Little Mermaid. This was very tough to watch. My wife and I were both shaken and hurt. The effect of European domination had never been so prominent in our home.

A quiet battle ensued. Baby Girl reached to undo her hair and I promptly advised her not to ruin what her mother spent countless hours doing. I assured her she looked beautiful and that Black women have different hair that is unique and amazing. In addition, I had to explain to her that Cinderella was not real and she should never aspire to look like someone so average. I continued to explain that Black women are blessed to be able to wear their hair in all kinds of styles. As tears continued to run down her face, I could see that none of this was making an impact. She wanted out of that hair, and she wanted out NOW. Her brother joined in our pleas to help Baby Girl understand how beautiful she looked. He told her she looked great, a hard feat for any brother to do. In the end, Baby Girl was not having it. I had to fix this immediately.

I got on the Internet and I said, "Do you know why I love see-

to question their own beauty before they are even aware of what is happening."

ing your hair like that?" She shook her head in silence through the tears. "Come here and sit on my lap," I said softly. She cautiously and with open disdain sat on my lap. I explained, "Because you look like that pretty lady from *The Matrix*." You see, my son and Baby Girl love *The Matrix*; they spend immeasurable hours watching Jada and crew rip up the screen. Although clearly neither of them get the plot, to watch people fly through the air and kick people in the chest makes for good film watching!

Anyway, as she cried with her head in her hands, I was on Google looking for *Matrix* photos. BAM!! I found Jada Pinkett-Smith strapped with gats looking all ladyfied and serious. I said, "See, Baby Girl, you are beautiful, like this lady in *The Matrix*. You are strong and smart and beautiful like she is. So, when Mommy made your hair like this it was because you remind us of a strong beautiful Black woman much like her."

Suddenly her face changed. It was amazing, and scary at first, to see how quickly a young woman can react to images in the media. Her self-confidence was at a new level. Her chin raised and the spine straightened. She slid off my lap and went back to look at herself in the full-length mirror in her brother's room. It was quiet back there. I sat in silence, totally excited, hoping I had made my point—but still scared.

Then I heard her going through her brother's stuff. Baby Girl came down the hall with a water gun, took the same pose as Niobi in the photo, and said, "FREEZE!! You are under arrest. This is the Matrix!" We all laughed. She immediately began to chase her brother through the house. Her smile was bright and full. Her laughter was real. My Baby Girl was back.

I want to thank Jada Pinkett-Smith and Lady of Rage for saving my daughter's self-esteem. Many American Black women lack a popular Black woman out there to raise their self-esteem. How many women have fallen for the Black hair matrix? How many young beautiful African American girls have destroyed themselves inside and out in pursuit of "the bluest eye?"

Nothing my wife or I might have said that day had the same great impact that Jada's photos had. So, Jada, thank you for being strong and for playing a character who can help young women feel good about themselves and their unique looks. Thank you to *The Matrix*

producers for creating a character who greatly influences the lives of these young women. Most importantly, thank you for helping us out of a situation that we wish had never been. Every girl should feel good about herself no matter what her hair, eyes, or skin look like, and sometimes a girl just needs someone to remind her that she is beautiful.

So, Jada, thank you for being that nonparental image that affirms, "You are beautiful and strong."

■

Down the Aisle,
Walkin' the Walk

▶ THABITI BOONE

Every father dreams of the day and opportunity to walk his daughter down the aisle on her wedding day and place her into the hands of a wonderful man who will honor, respect, and continue the love of his legacy. Saturday, June 2, 2007, my fatherhood dream became real. This dream was extra special. Against the odds, twenty-three years ago, in 1984, I decided at the age of nineteen to "walk the walk," to take responsibility as a man and be a responsible father; in some ways I was doing the unthinkable. I managed to balance the commitment and responsibilities of fatherhood, basketball stardom, education, and student activism. As a basketball star and single father, I took my daughter with me to college, and had to sacrifice my hoop dreams to raise her. When the church doors finally opened with Kim and I standing at the entrance, you could feel the earth separate and heaven begin to open up. The church was filled with family, friends, and loved ones, including

Kim's ten-month-old son Kingston, my first grandson. They were all standing with anticipation of your normal down-the-aisle-wedding walk. Aside from Kim being born, this was the proudest moment of my life. As Kim and I prepared to walk, we could feel each other's heartbeat. My entire body wept underneath my suit with pride and joy. Tears welled up in Kim's eyes. I felt her buckle with nervousness. She leaned over and said, "Daddy, I need you to hold me. I'm scared and ready to faint." I replied, "I got you, don't worry, I won't let you fall, just follow my lead." Once again, I had to step up. Daddy had to be there, to get his daughter through this precious moment. Holding her by the arm, walking down the aisle became more than just a wedding walk. It was a fatherhood journey. A journey filled with impossibility, challenge, and triumph.

My journey began during the rise of one of the most compelling musical genres of our times: Hip-Hop. By the '80s, New York City, particularly the South Bronx and East New York/Brownsville, Brooklyn, where I grew up, were seen as wastelands, desolate neighborhoods that trapped more dreams than they allowed out. These were neighborhoods where drugs, gangs, crime, violence, death, unemployment, poverty, public housing, inadequate schools and social programs, standing on street corners, and fatherless homes ruled. Concerns of fatherhood, positive male images, and the survival of urban youth were an afterthought.

My life nearly had a devastating beginning. I was born out of the statutory rape of a thirteen-year-old girl (my mother) by my twenty-two-year-old street-hustling father. (My fate was almost decided by a courthouse judge who suggested institutionalizing me, but my grandmother's prayers and pleas to have her grandson given to her—because her daughter was too young and my father didn't

▸ [Thabiti and daughter on her wedding day . . . walking that walk]

want the responsibility—helped save me.) I grew up watching my mother's young life get beat out of her everyday from the physical and emotional abuse of my father; witnessing, at the age of twelve, her breakdown and attempted suicide by jumping off the six-story rooftop of the housing project where we lived; and battling the system that tried to separate us. Also devastating was the untimely death of my daughter's mother, a death that prompted my child to claim that any hopes of a mother-and-daughter relationship were now killed. This was the world Kim and I were born into. Grandmaster Flash and the Furious Five said it best: "It's like a jungle sometimes . . . makes me wonder how I keep from going under."

Hip-Hop was born as a musical force connected to a social, cultural, and political agenda that would keep us from goin' under. I was a part of the coming-of-age second generation of Hip-Hop with a brand new Hip-Hop baby. The energy, power, and influence of Hip-Hop became one of my tools of inspiration to succeed as a single father, to not go under. I was determined to make it. I decided to be one less so-called nigga that institutional racism would keep in its so-called urban jungle.

In the delivery room, I waited for Kim's arrival into the world, relieved to know that no matter what happened, what challenges life threw at me, I was going to find a way to win, to always be there for her. With all that I'd gone through, I vowed to not become another father who refused to "walk the walk" for his child. I committed myself to walkin' the walk, to go down the aisle of life, to be a real man, a real father, to add my name to the distinguished scroll of honor of proud, dignified men and fathers.

Soon after Kim was born, things broke down between her mother and me. I was now a single father with a dilemma: Give Kim up to continue my NBA hoop dreams or take her with me to college. I decided to take her with me and take my chances.

I wasn't sure my dream was realistic. It was hard enough for inner-city young African-American men to dream and believe they could attend and complete college and have success. To do it with a baby, most people, including family, relatives, friends, and college officials thought I was crazy. Ghetto dreams of hope boiled down to selling dope, hangin' on street corners, gettin' over, or learning a killa crossover on the basketball courts. Black success beyond basketball courts and street corners never came back to show us how the grass was greener and hip on the other side. Rap became another game in town. It didn't require a degree for success. Biggie rapped, "If it wasn't for the rap game, I'd probably have a knee deep in the crack game 'cause the streets is a short stop, either you slingin' crack, rock, or you got a wicked jump shot." I wasn't a hustler or rapper. I was a basketball star. I got good grades, but ball was the way to get paid.

I arrived at college with little money, no fatherhood programs, nor available government services. Welfare even turned me down. I remember the agency worker at the window asking me "Where is this child's mother? How did you get her? Sorry, I can't help you." I thought, "How am I going to do this?" I had to get a game plan. With Hip-Hop moving toward consciousness, self-empowerment, and activism, I used it as my soundtrack for self-determination.

My support system included my mother, sister, brother, homeboys, students, sorority sisters, fraternity brothers, and most of all, my college girlfriend, Michelle, who became the mother Kim never had. They all kept me encouraged. I had to keep my basketball bouncing to the beat of maintaining my athletic scholarship so I could keep money and other resources for our food and living expenses coming in. KRS-One rapping, "You Must Learn" kept me on point with my books. To the beat of basketball and hip hop my fatherhood got into a groove. The groove lasted through boxes of diapers, hair braiding, baby baths, baby bottles, meals, late nights studying with me holding her in my lap, her first stroller ride, first bike, first day of school, homework, doctor visits, dance recitals, her first interest in boys, womanhood, high school, prom night, graduation, the death of her mother, college, motherhood, and marriage. For me, the groove lasted throughout my being president of the student union, graduating from college, giving my law degree to my mother, and helping her get a house.

That groove, the beat of the bouncing ball, also played during one of my darkest moments. I remember sitting alone in the locker room after my last college game. I had scored twenty-eight points, earning All-Star honors, but depression had kicked in. For the first time, I felt it was finally over. I could no longer handle the emotional battle between basketball and my daughter. Basketball and fatherhood were at opposite sides. I painfully gave up my love for basketball for the choice of loving and raising my daughter—something the NBA's millions could never do. Queen Latifah's anthem was "Ladies First." Kim had to be first in my life.

Walking Kim down the aisle was the greatest point I ever scored. She taught me that while basketball was a part of my life, it was not the complete purpose of it. She also taught me that basketball was more than just a game. It was my way out. But it wasn't my life; she was. I got Kim down the aisle. Everyone knew she was my life and I would always walk with her.

Fathers, go down the aisle of life with your children. Walk with them. They can't make it without you. As Public Enemy said, "It takes a nation of millions to hold us back."

■

Poems
by Saddi Khali

▸ **FATHERLESS CHILD (29 YEARS LATER)**

at 31
i am forced
to create
an image
of manhood
for which i
have only

magic in
a world of
smoke and mirrors

▸ OUR FATHER

Our father who art in absence
Hollow be thy frame
Thou left thy son
Why hath thou done such hurt?
We have to ask this question
Give us this say that is rarely said
& just give us more chances
as we forgive them that got ass & left us.
And lead us not by past example
But deliver cuz we need u
For thine intervention adds a power to the story
whenever
A man.

▸ YOUR SON

I am your son
A male raised in a manless home
My mother was my father
The story of my childhood is a torn piece of cloth
My memories dangle like string

The radio was my father
Songs divorced from love
separated from life
were my relationship blueprints
I became a dj in a crowded club of girls
Makin short skirts & halters
dance to a hit song called
"We don't love them hoes"
I am alone, now
No one told me I could change the station

I am your son

A male raised in a manless home
Television was my father
"calling all cars, calling all cars"
"mr. mcgee, don't make me angry
    you wouldn't like me when I'm angry"
"ok, u wanna go to war? I'll take u to war"
    I fought my whole life like life depended on it
Fighting is all I really know how to do

The corner of the block was my father
Where young men w/
Battle-scarred schemes & caviar dreams
get thrown to the pavement
like dice

I am your son
A male raised in a manless home
I was my own father
Taking manhood ingredients
From my mother, the radio, the tv, the corner
I am the gumbo of what I've seen
For anyone who wonders if I will
ever raise a child into a man
tell them, I already have

■

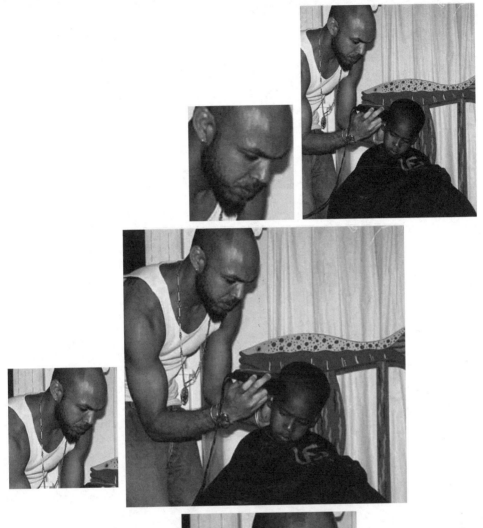

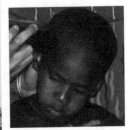

Truth and
Reconciliation

▶ KEVIN WILLIAMS

"Actions have reactions, don't be quick to judge
You may not know the hardships people don't speak of
It's best to step back and observe with couth
For we all must meet our moment of truth
—Guru, "Moment of Truth" (1998)

Apartheid: A legal policy of racial segregation formerly practiced in South Africa involving political, social, and economic discrimination against nonwhite people. After almost fifty years of rule, apartheid ended in 1993 and the people of South Africa held truth and reconciliation hearings. They wanted information about the systems of oppression, kidnappings, and murders committed on behalf of the government so that they could move forward. Recently, I spent sixteen days in South Africa listening to people's stories of life under apartheid. They spoke of how they were able to move on. It forced me to reassess a personal situation I was currently embattled with: the custody and child support of my daughter I was raising. "How could I not forgive?" Compared to what I had just learned from the people of South Africa, my fatherhood issues seemed so small.

South Africa's apartheid was the current event news of the day when my daughter Shantel was born. I was nineteen and attending Howard University in Washington, D.C. Hip-hop was in what is now called the golden era. Public Enemy and KRS-One helped me understand the world I was living in. I was a student activist trying to do something positive with my life, but I was not equipped for fatherhood—mentally or financially. As a fulltime college student, I did my best. I worked six days a week and spent the seventh day with Shantel, who also lived in D.C. with her mother (my former girlfriend) Simone. Simone and I had agreed that I would pay half of Shantel's expenses. The worries of making ends meet kept me awake at night. Little did I know that these worries were just the tip of the iceberg.

**The situation that I'm facin', is mad amazing
to think such problems can arise from minor confrontations.
—Guru, "Moment of Truth"**

It all started when I was too tired to talk to Simone one night after work. She got angry and we had a big argument. A few weeks later, I got a letter from District of Columbia Child Support Services.

My first appearance in family court was heard in an open court-room with zero privacy. I, along with the other fathers, had to tell our stories in front of everyone else. The mothers, however, did not even have to appear (D.C. government provides them with a lawyer known as Corporation Counsel). After courthouse formalities, I was

asked standard questions, such as "Do you attest the child is yours?" I was told that if I wish to have a paternity test and the results prove I am the father, I would have to pay $400. There is no mention of cost if the mother was wrong. I sit patiently. Eventually I am called before a judge. I begin: "Your Honor, I am currently unemployed. I had a contract job with an accounting firm that ended, but I was able to save enough money to pay for my daughter's care while I search for employment. I have one year left before I graduate from Howard University. I currently pay half of my daughter's expenses at $205 each month. I am prepared to continue those payments while I search for employment." The judge applauds all my efforts, and then sends me and Simone off to speak with a child support worker. The three of us review childcare expenses, but a support order cannot be placed because I am unemployed. The worker, who knows that I am a fulltime student, forces me to report before the judge every week until I find a job. Unbelievable! I cannot afford to miss an entire day of class every week until I am employed. The main point has been missed: I already pay half of my daughter's expenses. I sign the papers regardless, thereby agreeing to continue to make payments and continue to seek employment. My next court date is scheduled and I'm told that if I miss that date a warrant can be made for my arrest.

Several times a week, I reported to an employment office—one that primarily lists fulltime positions. With twelve months left to graduate, I was not willing to turn my back on the long-term benefits of a college degree in favor of a short-term remedy from a clueless child support worker.

Sometimes you gotta dig deep, when problems come near
Don't fear. Things get severe for everybody everywhere
Why do bad things happen, to good people?
Seems that life is just a constant war between good and evil.
—Guru, "Moment of Truth"

My second court date brought a new judge that told me I might have to quit college in order to find a job. Suddenly I'm labeled a deadbeat dad, despite that fact that I continued my payments while searching for work. I started to pick up the newspapers' early editions at 2:00 AM just to get a jump on the competition. Eventually, I found a job just before my third court appearance. At the appearance, the judge congratulates me and schedules another court date. My payments will be determined after I receive several paychecks.

While waiting for my final support order, Simone asks me to bypass the system and pay her directly. With that, she would drop the child support case, she promised. She asked this of me because the time between my payment to the child support office and her receipt of the check was taking too long. This was creating problems and Shantel's daycare threatened to put her out. I opted to pay the center directly, but Simone did not drop the case. In the meantime, the court mistakenly garnished double the temporary support order amount. Before all this is corrected, I was in my own financial bind. I borrowed money from friends and strongly considered making money illegally with some old associates.

At my fourth court date, things finally began to turn around. The District of Columbia asked for more money than I was required to pay. The same judge who suggested I quit school asked for my thoughts on this. I replied that I would pay the minimum amount for as long as this case remained in the courts, but if Simone drops the case, I would continue to pay half of my daughter's expenses. The judge then reprimanded Corporation Counsel for not understanding what was in the best interest of the child and dismissed the case.

Be a father, if not, why bother, son
A boy can make 'em, but a man can raise one
If you did it, admit it and stick with it
—Ed O.G. "Be a Father to Your Child"

While society is generally patriarchal, child support is certainly a matriarchal system. I was reminded of that four months after I graduated from college. I had Shantel come live with me in Washington D.C. before we moved to New York City, where I would begin a career with the Department of Education. After less than $1,000 of support in eight years and threats of a custodial fight, it was time to make things official. The courts granted me sole custody and established the agreement quickly. Next, I sought child support payments. Simone's financial report indicated that she should pay $380 per month. The hearing's examiner, however, asked her how much she could afford and she said $250 per month. So, it was ordered—just like that. Outraged, I appealed. A higher court reset the amount to $380. This time Simone appealed, citing the birth of a new child as reason she could not pay more. Again, the amount was reduced to $250 per month. There was nothing I could do about it.

The disrespect continued while I fought to receive money for my daughter. On one such occasion, I hadn't received any child support payments because the Division of Child Support Enforcement lost my paperwork when I moved from one county to another. One official told me to stop moving. Another refused to help because he said that fathers had to prove custody if they were receiving child support payments from mothers (women, on the other hand, never have to prove custody in order to receive support from men). Ultimately, I had to contact a New York State deputy commissioner of child support in order to reestablish my child support payments. That took nine months.

We gon' make it, we gon' make it, we gon' make it.
—Jadakiss

Over the years, I have tried unsuccessfully to get over my anger, but my experience with the double standard of the child support system has left me bitter. The sting of being told to quit school, facing the prospect of being arrested, having never received any automatic cost-of-living adjustments, and having never received an apology for the mishandling and delay of my records, which triggered crippling financial hardships, is still being felt. I thought my visit to South Africa was going to be the beginning of the healing process, but once I returned home, I realized I was not ready. I understand that in South Africa, truth and reconciliation did not start *before* apartheid ended; so at home I know that before healing can begin, the damage must stop. Right now, I am still fighting within an oppressive child support system that has little regard for fathers. Though I am battle-weary and scarred, I love being a father to my daughter and I am proud of the woman she has become.

■

Do the Sons Bear the Sins of the Father?

▸ DION CHAVIS

When experiencing the death of a parent most
people go through extreme grief. My dad's
name was Elbert Parker, but all of his close
friends and family called him "Bunny." When
my father was shot and killed in February of
1991 I didn't experience any immediate pain.
As a child, I had been forced to spend every
other weekend with my father as a part of a
court-ordered custody and visitation. It was
never something that I looked forward to.
His house was filthy, I had to sleep on the
couch, there was always some random ani-
mal strolling around, and all pops seemed
to be worried about was who my mom was
dating. Every other weekend I was forced to

pretend I was having a good time and enjoying people around me who I hardly knew. I tried my best not to show my discontent with the visitation while with him, but as a child it was hard for me to grasp the "grin and bear it" attitude. Especially when Bunny's mom couldn't even remember my real name. She would always say things like "Hey Donnie" or "Come here, Donnie." In my mind I would be thinking, "Lady, my name is Dion."

Due to Bunny's alcoholism and recreational cocaine use, my mom decided to leave him when I was three years old. It wasn't just the everyday consumption of malt liquor or the sniffing of those all-too-familiar white lines that led her to leave. It was the verbal abuse that she refused to tolerate. Bunny had a temper, a bad temper. When he would get inebriated he would kick down doors, punch holes in walls, go to work drunk, and curse out his supervisor. You name it, and Elbert Parker probably did it.

Bunny had an "anybody can get it" type of attitude. Unfortunately, I think that it was this particular way of thinking that caused him to meet his death on his thirty-fifth birthday. He got into an argument with two men one day. During the argument he savagely punched and choked one of the men almost to the point of unconsciousness. After the altercation the two men fled. Later that evening, Bunny went out to celebrate his birthday. When he returned home, the two men approached him again. This time they had guns, and they were ready to retaliate. After a brief argument, my father was shot several times. He was critically injured and died a few hours later in the hospital.

I don't know what affected me more, my father's death or his lack of parental involvement while he was alive. Here I am, an eleven-year-old kid being raised by a single mother who was working three jobs. Some people who were in similar situations were sucked in by the streets and turned to a life of violence and drugs. Some were blessed with great athletic ability and used sports as a way to make a difference for themselves. I was never into the street life, and at best I was average in a few sports. So, without any dominating male figure in my life I turned to the one thing that I knew would always be there, Hip Hop.

Even though my mother was there to guide me through those rough adolescent and teenage years without the help of a male counterpart, there are some things that a woman just cannot teach her son. I didn't have anyone to teach me life lessons from a male's point of view. I felt closest to those men on the television and on the radio who represented what I loved. I learned from them, I laughed at them, I taught their messages to others. It was Big Daddy Kane who taught me the ins and outs of being a fast-talking city slicker. With his "Smooth Operator" attitude, Kane paved the way for the "grown man" styles of many of today's popular artists. Rappers such as KRS-One, Public Enemy, and Poor Righteous Teachers schooled me on Black history. The teachings and messages that uplifted people mixed with the infectious boom bap of the '90s beat machines left me thirsting to know more about my culture and where it came from. So through it all, whenever I needed to get a better understanding of something from a

male's point of view, I knew that the music and culture of Hip Hop would be there to keep me informed, as well as entertained. Elbert Parker may have contributed to my conception, but it was the creators and contributors of Hip Hop who get the props for teaching me the things that my mother couldn't.

The culture of Hip Hop helped define my upbringing, but when it was time for me to be a father I knew that I had to step up to the plate and take full responsibility. In June of 2004 when my daughter Nyla was born, I was a twenty-three-year-old young man who didn't know the first thing about raising a child.

Nyla's mother Latrice and I only dated for a few months before she became pregnant. As with most relationships that move along too fast, things between Latrice and I just didn't work out. While she was pregnant I realized that we were two totally different types of people. She was one of those people who looked at life as "my way or the highway." Being a smart-mouthed, always-have-to-have-the-last-word, quick-tempered, and moody Gemini, I couldn't handle the constant personality clashes. Latrice and I decided to call it quits when she was six months pregnant. In my mind, there was no need to stick around in a situation where both people are miserable and you just know in your heart that it isn't going to work.

"In my heart I knew that I could

never g

"I'll never give **ive up** on my daughter because my mother never gave up on me."

Once Nyla was born, I knew that no matter what happened I was going to be a part of her life. I couldn't count on anyone else to give my daughter the guidance that she needed to grow into a responsible young woman. So from day one, I did anything and everything to make sure that I stayed in Nyla's life, regardless of what happened between her mother and I.

For the next three years, Latrice and I fought some of the hardest knock-down, drag-out battles, both in and out of court. I encountered verbal threats, false accusations of child abuse, not being able to speak to Nyla on the phone, and many other unthinkable actions. I pretty much went through it all. There were times that I wanted to give up. I asked myself every day "How could a mother claim to love a child but do everything in her power to keep the child's father away from them?" On some occasions I even asked myself if I was being punished for the transgressions that my father committed while he was living.

But there was one thing that Hip Hop never taught me: "Hell hath no fury like a woman scorned." In my heart I knew that I could never give up on my daughter because my mother never gave up on me. She fought stereotypes and defied the odds to make sure that she gave me the best life that she possibly could. It was that same strength and fortitude that drove me to do whatever I had to do to make sure that I was always a part of Nyla's life. Eventually, through patience and prayer, Latrice and I were able to act like adults and put our differences behind us.

So today, as a man who grew up without a father, I am doing everything in my power to make sure that I am here to raise my child. Times have changed, and the messages in most of today's music don't line up with the morals and values that are required to raise a child. I have to be there for my daughter as much as I possibly can. As a child of Hip Hop and a child of the struggle, it is my duty to make sure that she has the core values of the culture instilled in her. The music has changed, the images are more graphic, but the culture is still the same. Hip Hop is something that will live inside of me forever, in the way that I walk, talk, speak, and think. It's funny watching Nyla grow up because I see so many of the characteristics that make me who I am inside of her. I know that I could have done so many things differently in my life. But when it comes to raising my child in today's world I think a lyric from Mos Def sums it up the best: "I ain't no perfect man/I'm tryin' to do the best that I can/with what it is I have."

G-Daddy: A Father's Rage; A Grandfather's Delight

▸   MO BEASLEY

"Daddy, I'm pregnant." I was thirty-six when my then nineteen-year-old daughter, Tanya, dropped this news near the end of her freshman year at Spelman College. I was frightened, outraged, and I felt defeated. Tanya and her mother responded with common replies for this common situation. They embraced the pregnancy with pledges of "We're gonna' do whatever we gotta' do to take care of this baby." Tanya's mother, my ex-girlfriend Leslie, added, "I did it, and she can do it, too." Today, I am the forty-year-old grandfather of an adorable four-year-old named Vanessa. My journey to fatherhood and grandfatherhood has been like no other.

My mother was unmarried and seventeen when she had me. Leslie and I were seventeen and unmarried when we had Tanya. Tanya was nineteen and unmarried when she had Vanessa. This cycle is all too common with poor Black families, including my family in Boston. Maybe this cycle is common because sex is more than about procreation, or recreation for that matter. Perhaps "babies having babies" is common because sex is often an escape from despair, not unlike drugs and alcohol.

It is also common that teenage mothers do the child raising in the family . . . *solo*. When I was an adult and asked my father why he didn't spend more time with me as a child, he replied, "The women raise the children." His absence became my subconscious model of how *not* to father. My Uncle Reuben, a major father figure of my childhood, preached to me and all my male cousins: "Drop as many seeds as you can, that's your legacy to leave so muthafuckas know you was here. It's their mothers' jobs to clothe and feed." I have never believed their creeds because I knew, intimately, the pains of single mothers and fatherless children. It was an experience that I, and most of the children I grew up with, knew too well.

Growing up on welfare during the late '60s, early '70s, my family was victim to social service home invasions by social workers who would search our homes regularly for evidence of a man in the household. That would have implied that a family didn't need public assistance. If there was any evidence that a man lived with us, then our welfare checks and food stamps were in jeopardy. As a child in Boston, I was also introduced to the connec-

tion between race and class. I would watch news reports that profiled poor Irish or Italian families with a mother, children, *and a father in the home.* That white family could publicly ask for government aid and get it, without penalty! The double standards that undermine black fatherhood, then and now, outrage me still.

Racial tension and poverty was my backdrop growing up. Hustling weed, dropping out of high school, and fathering babies with different women was the norm for most young men in my community. I ran from that lifestyle with the desperation of a slave seeking freedom. Other men were content to get high, get laid, get paid, and get by. I, on the other hand, had to get away from that quagmire before I got sucked into it—angry and unfulfilled like most of the dads I knew. I had to go even if it meant leaving my baby girl for a while. At seventeen, I had become a father before I became a man. I also knew that I could provide more for my daughter as a college graduate than as a security guard (my job after high school).

So I left Beantown on a one-way train to Washington, D.C.—headed to Howard University. My father actually encouraged me to follow my dream and pursue a degree in theater arts, despite the fact that the arts

didn't pay much. He knew my passion. I was a '70s child growing up on the soul music of my daddy's records: James Brown, Curtis Mayfield, and Marvin Gaye. Hip-Hop was prominent while I was in school, but it never moved me as deeply as soul music. Hip-Hop disappointed me. With the exception of Public Enemy and KRS-One, it wasn't serious enough for a kid running from his ghetto demons. It sampled the music of our parents' era, but not the message. The explosion of gangsta rap spoke to the brothers I grew up with and who were still trying to survive post–Civil Rights/Vietnam War/Black Power fallout. The Hip-Hop of the late '80s/early '90s pointed me to the streets I was running from with every college credit that I earned. Hip-Hop wanted to glorify ghetto living but my hustle wasn't connected to promoting our problems. I had a little girl to support.

I managed to graduate from college and struggled every minute to make a better life for Tanya and me. When she was fifteen and her *wildin out* had exhausted her mom and step-dad, I moved her from Boston to New York (where I had moved). It was the first time I took a job outside my chosen profession in live theater. Like most black mothers do (and many black fathers don't), I did whatever I had to do to take care of my daughter. For four years, as a single dad, I raised Tanya from her turbulent teenage years into adulthood. I challenged my troubled "woman-child" to reinvent herself by leaving old excuses and failures behind. She answered by taking extra classes and eventually upgraded her academic standing and became an honor student!

All this work was geared toward expanding past our humble beginnings. I thought all the personal sacrifice had paid off. Tanya was accepted to Spelman, the premier institution of higher learning for African-American women. This, I thought, was going to be

the beginning of a new family legacy.

I agree with Chris Rock: I don't deserve praise for doing what I am supposed to do as a father, but I reserve the right to be outraged when I busted my ass to give my daughter a solid grip on life, only for her to let it go by getting pregnant before she's able to care for herself or her child. I felt betrayed. Why was an unplanned pregnancy an option for Tanya? Why did my family take this in stride, and why was I trippin' so hard?

> ### "My mother was unmarried and seventeen when she had me."

The cycle of single, teenage parenthood swept across my door when we were so close to shutting it out. I was tripping not just off my situation, but also off mothers who don't have the courage to tell their daughters that seeking unconditional love in the arms of a baby, to fill emotional voids, is a fool's pursuit. I was also angry with myself for not giving my daughter more emotional, spiritual, and financial support in the early part of her life. And I have always been outraged about fathers who do "hit and runs" against women and leave their children longing.

Now that four years have passed, I have calmed down. I reflect on the words of poet Kahlil Gibran: "Your children are not your children, they are the sons and daughters of life's longing for itself, they come through you but they are not from you . . . strive to be like them but you cannot make them just like you." It is the creed I parent by; a creed I shared with Tanya on her fifteenth birthday. It reminds me that projecting my wishes onto my daughter may have left her little room to conjure a life of her own imaginings. I had hoped that Tanya's drive to turn her life around would be enough to carry her through the culture shock of going to college in an environment so different from that of her childhood. In hindsight, it may have been too much of a jolt to Tanya's foundation. Just when life with Daddy started to make sense, it was time to leave and build another world, at nineteen. Motherhood at such a young age is not what I hoped for her, but perhaps she sought comfort in its familiarity—like her mother and grandmother before her.

Tanya and Vanessa returned home to Leslie in Boston. Admittedly, I am still afraid for the future of my family and poor Black families like us. But I also enjoy what is. I am learning to release my fears, to focus on the joy that my daughters bring me. I envision a future that brings them happiness and I enjoy being "G-Daddy," as my granddaughter calls me.

Through my craft, I also seek to challenge this common thinking within our community. If more daddies and mommies stay in the struggle to raise our children *together*, then we build stronger family units and healthier communities. As long as I stay in my daughters' lives—focused on the positive and working to eradicate the negative, then my family will thrive, not just survive. That is this G-Daddy's delight.

■

Who's The Man?

▸ CHEO TYEHIMBA

During the summer of 1979, like most fourteen-year-old boys I spent most of my time thinking about one thing: girls. We'd been sitting in the front seat of a Mack truck parked on the block. Our voices were boisterous, full of the kind of teenage shit-talk used by boys searching for manhood.

"Maaan, did you see her in that tube top?" I nudged Cornell, my best friend since the sixth grade.

"Yeah, I thought it was gonna fall off!" he said. "Girl's a *hammer*, man, you hear me? *Daddy Mack* might have to step to that . . ."

"Yeah, right" I laughed. "You know I'm the man. You just a squirrel trying to get a nut! Besides, Denitra is at least nineteen and she ain't thinkin' 'bout yo ass. Plus, you know Black Rock don't play that."

Black Rock was Denitra's dad and the neighborhood pimp. Not the kind of "pimp" who runs women, but that Seventies archetype of well-tailored, smooth-talking Black Macho that women noticed and men envied. He drove a truck for a living ("Black Rock" was his CB handle) and he worked when he wanted. He had a two-story house, always drove a late-model car, and allowed many of the neighborhood kids to swim in his pool during the summer. He was a jovial, dark-skinned brother with goose-egg eyes—kind of a taller, happier James Baldwin. While he played "bones," drank gin, and entertained friends poolside, we used his place as the neighborhood teen center. I didn't realize it then, but inviting us to his place was also his way to keep his eye on the boys who were interested in his teenage daughter.

Also unbeknownst to me then, Black Rock sold drugs on my block during the early eighties, for which he was ultimately arrested. Thinking about it now, I am absolutely sure Black Rock and his flashy crew of "Players Ball"-styled friends used drugs too—marijuana and cocaine were never in short supply. But this is not a story about Black Rock the criminal. This is a story about the only visible black man with a semblance of power living on my block when I was fourteen and what it taught me about manhood, and ultimately fatherhood.

We lived in East San Jose, CA, a working-class Bay Area community struggling in the shadows of the area's then-burgeoning Silicon Valley computer industry. While

elationship with my if not nonexistent."

young, privileged white kids invented personal computers in their garages (i.e., the HP and Apple Computer empires) a few miles away, crack cocaine flooded our neighborhoods. This was documented by the late San Jose *Mercury News* reporter Gary Webb, whose 1996 investigative series "Dark Alliance" reported that the CIA backed the Contras

(Nicaraguan revolutionaries) who had distributed crack cocaine into Black communities in both Los Angeles and the Bay Area, in order to funnel profits to aid the Contras' ongoing war with the Sandinistas. Of course, at the time I could never know that this complex web would spawn the crack epidemic that still plagues us today.

By the time I somehow figured out a way to leave my block for college, I would be thoroughly immersed in a political cauldron in which the music and culture of the "Golden Age" of Hip Hop permanently influenced my uncompromising political ideas. We flocked to films like *Breakin'* and *Krush Groove*, mimicked rappers to hone our skills at doing "the dozens," and derived our defiant, cool pose from groups like Run DMC, KRS-One, Eric B. & Rakim, N.W.A., and Public Enemy. In fact, Public Enemy's "It Takes a Nation of Millions to Hold Us Back" was probably the closest thing to a coming-of-age soundtrack for my generation. It helped create a culture that emphasized "knowledge of self." Sporting high-top fades; red, black, and green Africa medallions; and gold rope chains around our necks, we pumped our fists while screaming "Fight the Power" at Free South Africa rallies. Hip hop gave us context for what time it was in America.

I knew nothing then of the complex social and economic forces in the world that conspired against people like me. What I *did* know is that I had no one in my life besides my two older brothers to show me what being a black man was all about. And since they weren't yet men themselves, we all faked it. My parents had divorced when I was three, so my ideas of what men (and fathers) did or could do, mostly came from thin air.

Like most of the black men of my generation, my relationship

"Like most of the bla absent father was te

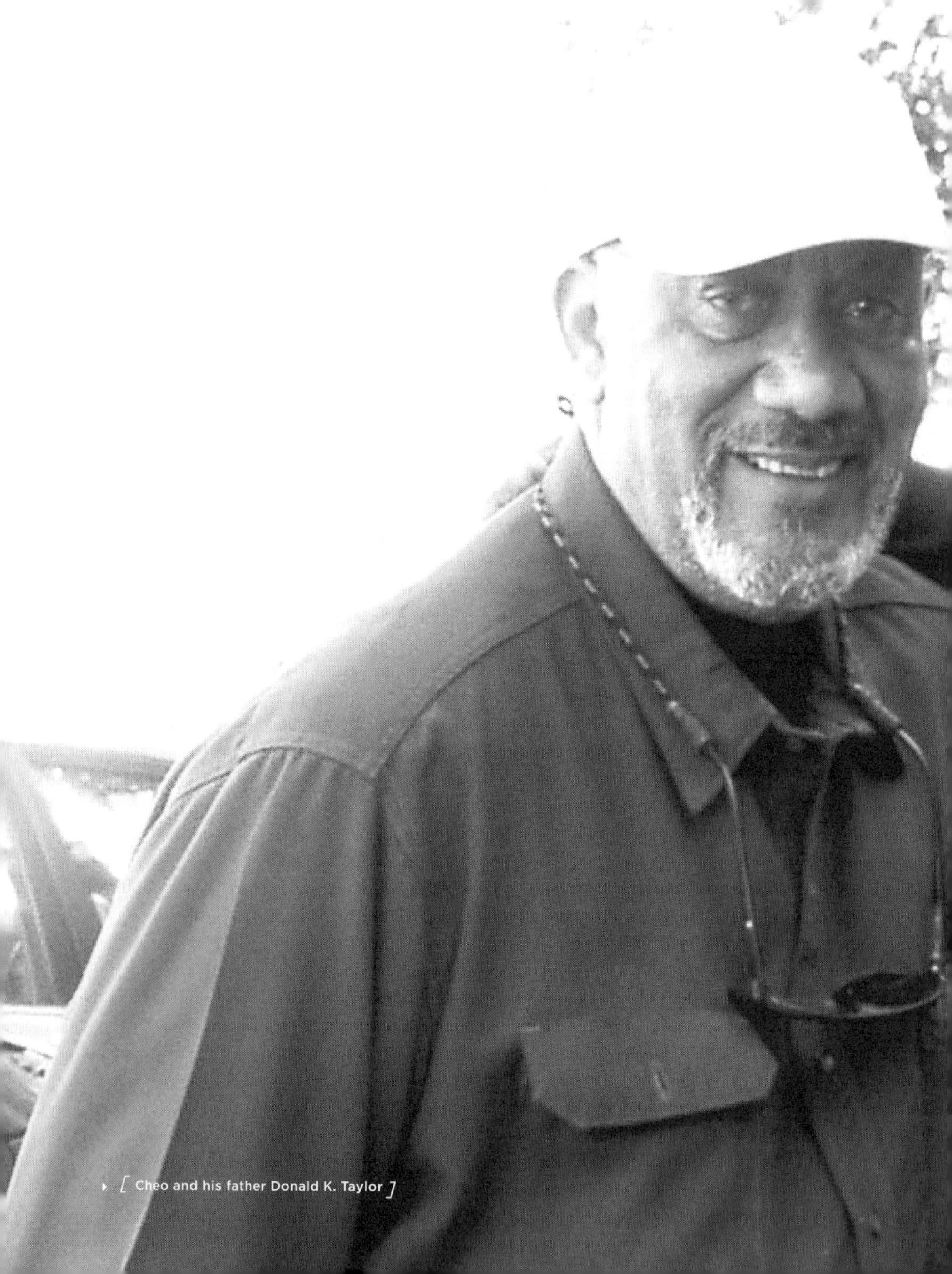

[Cheo and his father Donald K. Taylor]

with my absent father was tenuous, if not nonexistent. By the time I reached adolescence, I began to closely watch any black man I encountered for clues. Black Rock played his position, I learned to played mine. The lessons? Being a black man was measured by how much shit one could talk, how much money one made, how many women one could conquer, and how much pain one could inflict or withstand.

But those lessons had a cost. The night Black Rock was arrested his daughter Denitra came by our house. We peeked from behind the curtains just in time to see the police walking Black Rock away in handcuffs. She was scared, but absolute in her belief in his "sainthood." I never saw Black Rock again, but I'll never forget how Denitra spoke of her father with such reverence and admiration. It was a bond I'd wished I had with my own father, who, at the time, had just moved back in with us after more than a decade.

My parents decided to remarry, which in theory seemed to be a great thing. But since I only had about two years left in high school, his return, at least in my mind, felt too little, too late. I rebelled. We argued. It was a hard adjustment, having someone show up and ask to be respected when many of the things they'd done in the past didn't warrant respect. By the time I went away to college our relationship was still fragile.

It took at least another ten years for my relationship with my father to really evolve and become as strong as it is today. A lot of that had to do with my own maturity and our understanding of why things happened the way they did. I came to appreciate him for his strong intellect, charismatic personality, and independent views.

But it wasn't until he recently mailed me the "story of his life" that I had the rare occasion to learn more about the assorted details of how he fell down; how he lost his wife, kids, and bright career to alcoholism. After one too many letdowns, my mom left him—packed me and my two brothers on a train bound for Springfield, Massachusetts, to start over on the East Coast. Although he tried to find his way back to us a few times, he failed. He wasn't trying to be a "Cosby Dad" or didn't know how. He'd wanted to become a "serious writer" and didn't know what to do when he found himself with a wife and three kids. He would find success in the corporate world over and over again, breaking sales records and winning executive-level jobs, only to drink it all away. He was a dreamer who tried to jettison history itself; out, beyond the confines of what black men were allowed to do during that time. Finally, when they remarried, he rebuilt his career and learned to keep a job, learned to keep a promise. Of course by then, he had done a lot of growing up, too; he wasn't the twenty-year-old kid he was when they first married.

Today when I think back to those days hangin' out at Black Rock's house and how I used to look up to him it makes me pause. Was he "the Man"? I used to think so. In the absence of real men—men who know how to give and receive love, raise or mentor children, think independently, and be self-sustaining—any male will do.

So how do we *grow* black boys in America? Why are the most visible role models ones that reflect hyper-masculine, supersexist, patriarchal, and ultra-consumerist ways of life? Why are black men continuing to be "destroyed" as boys? I don't have all the answers. I just know that an ongoing, intergenerational relationship with a self-aware, self-loving black man (hopefully your father) is a great place to start.

My pops, Donald K. Taylor, has replaced lost time by finding himself, by being a father I can be proud of. He has become one of the most influential people in the making of who I am, "the man" I am today. His unexpected, unabashedly honest seventy-page autobiography is a profound gift to his son, one that I hope to be able to give to my son or daughter one day.

■

▶ ⎡ Che a/k/a Rhymefest and his son Solomon ⎤

An Interview
with Rhymefest

▶ RHYMEFEST IS WELL-KNOWN IN THE HIP HOP WORLD FOR THE GRAMMY
AWARD-WINNING SONG HE COWROTE WITH KANYE WEST, "JESUS WALKS," IN
2005. THE CHICAGO NATIVE IS EQUALLY KNOWN FOR HIS SHARP WIT
AND CUTTING-EDGE INSIGHTS. WITH HIS DEBUT ALBUM *BLUE COLLAR* (ALLIDO
RECORDS/J RECORDS) GETTING CRITICAL ACCLAIM AND HIS NEW ALBUM
EL CHE DUE IN 2008, RHYMEFEST CONTINUES TO STAY RELEVANT NOT JUST
IN THE WORLD OF MUSIC, BUT IN THE REALM OF SOCIAL ISSUES AS WELL.
OPINIONATED AND AS STRIKING AS EVER, THE RAPPER SHARES WITH ME SOME
OF HIS VIEWS ON THE TOPIC OF HIP HOP AND FATHERHOOD.

ARS: What does fatherhood mean to you, especially as it relates to African American men who came of age during the hip hop era?

Rhymefest: Fatherhood, as it relates to Black men in general, is a historically complex story about one of the most brutalized and insecure populations on earth. At one point, in [what was] our peculiar institution (slavery), Black families were forcibly ripped apart—so much so that the tradition of a dysfunctional family became a part of our psyche. However, due to historical power moves such as the Harlem Renaissance, the Black Power movement, and the Hip Hop generation, there is a reconnection that has taken place between fathers and sons that can't be stopped regardless of what the powers that be (white supremacy) place before us, i.e. drugs, media misinformation, and project prisons.

ARS: Some argue that hip hop's original generation is the "forsaken" generation—the one with the most strikes against it (i.e., the crack epidemic, high rates of fatherlessness, the growth of the prison-industrial complex, and so on). With all these things considered, would you say Black men (particularly those who came of age during hip hop's rise) triumphed over these ills or fell victim to them?

Rhymefest: I think that question is not a question that pertains to Black men in only the Hip Hop generation, but Black men historically of all generations. I think that it is very dangerous to associate a culture of music with fatherhood. Would we ask the question, Were fathers of the Motown era any less or more fathers because Marvin Gaye sung *Mercy Me* or Edwin Starr sung *War*? Did that provoke or prevent anything as far as how their children were raised? How can we then associate Master P's No Limit movement, or Tupac's Thug Movement, with how men are supposed to raise their own seeds? The question being asked is a trick question because fatherhood can only be determined by the content of the father's character.

ARS: Some argue that hip hop culture itself personified the "father figure" in many Black men's lives—filling in the role for many absentee dads. Would you agree with that assertion?

Rhymefest: It is definitely true that because of the directness of Hip Hop, the unapologetic statements that rappers make—we talk to you, we tell you what's in style, what's fake, what's real—we disseminate orders. We have even called for the assassination of other artists in the public eye, and yes, our children really see that shit happening. Tupac, Biggie, Big L—we are the unofficial authority in your home. Have we replaced real fathers? I guess that all depends on how powerful you believe real fathers can be.

ARS: Has your life as a popular hip hop artist positively or negatively impacted how you raise your child?

Rhymefest: Honestly, it has negatively impacted my child as far as the time that I am able to spend with him. There is an unhealthy relationship that my career has bred between my son's mother and I due to groupies, management, and misperceptions of wealth. This all impacts my child in a way that he may not understand until his teenage years. But hell, by then his maturity level will be developed and skewed in a way that may or may not be normal.

ARS: What are the key differences and similarities between how your father raised you and how you raise your son? If your father was not present in your life, was there a grandfather or father figure who served in a "fatherly" capacity?

Rhymefest: I, like many Black men in America, sought a father figure wherever I could, because my biological father was not present. I turned to gangs, friends, religious figures, and even media personalities (yes, rappers) and did what most people searching for God do: took a little piece of what I thought was good from each one, and molded myself in its image.

ARS: What four things do you think must happen in order for a generation of men who came of age during the hip hop era to create healthy relationships with their fathers and/or their daughters and sons?

Rhymefest: I don't know if we can number 1 thru 4 steps that can be taken in order to create healthy relationships with our families. Although, there are some commonsense things that can be done in any family—Hip Hop, White, Black, woman, man, or whatever—to foster strong ties and bonds that can't be broken.

#1—The existence of God, and or some kind of spiritual tradition within the family whereby everyone can believe in the same creator for the same purpose, with the same mission. That is unity. Unity is strength.

#2—The sharing of resources. When one member of a family is in need, the other members of the family step up to fulfill that need until said person can be strong enough to help another family member when necessary.

#3—We must all understand that because of the damage that has been done to the Black American traditional family, family for us has morphed into many different meanings. A child does not have to be a biological son to be your son. And by the same token, just because you live in the house with the same man you share blood with, doesn't necessarily mean that he is fulfilling his role as your father. Family, I think, should be defined as people who share a common bond, secure and protect each other in that bond, and selflessly give of themselves in order to grow as a unit. Strong family can transcend beyond blood, barriers, and borders.

Like I said, I don't know if there's a magic numerical placement of what defines the promotion of strong family, but I do know that within Black America, in Hip Hop culture, without family bonds we will all surely die.

ARS: What key things do you think black women and black mothers must understand about the state of black fatherhood among the hip hop community?

Rhymefest: Black mothers, I believe, must be patient with Black men and realize that many of their children's fathers did not have fathers. Therefore, they suffer from some of the same immaturities as the child. Specifically, Black women must make wiser decisions in terms of who they chose to procreate with. It is no coincidence that John Kerry married into the

Heinz family. Or that Arnold Schwarzenegger married into the Kennedy family. Black women must stop choosing their child's fathers from the club or at BlackPlanet.com, and create rich, intelligent children from rich, intelligent gene pools.

ARS: What key lessons of life have you learned from your father, if any? If there are lessons learned from him, do you believe you are effectively instilling those lessons in your child?

Rhymefest: None and no.

■

Because Of My Father . . .

▶ BYRON HURT

EDITOR'S NOTE: FOR THIRTY-EIGHT YEARS, JACKIE AND BYRON HURT SHARED
A VERY SPECIAL BOND AS FATHER AND SON. IN JUNE 2007, JACKIE HURT
DIED OF PANCREATIC CANCER. HE WAS DIAGNOSED IN 2004. (MOST PEOPLE WITH
THIS VERY AGGRESSIVE FORM OF CANCER PASS WITHIN THREE TO SIX MONTHS
AFTER DIAGNOSIS.) I WENT TO MR. HURT'S FUNERAL TO SHOW SUPPORT FOR THE
HURT FAMILY AND, AFTER HEARING BYRON'S REMARKS, I ASKED HIM TO
SUBMIT THOSE REMARKS FOR THIS ANTHOLOGY. THE FOLLOWING IS AN EXCERPT
OF A SON'S LOVING TRIBUTE AT HIS FATHER'S HOMECOMING SERVICE.

GOALS:

1. Do my father and his legacy justice.
2. Bring everyone in the church to his or her feet.
3. Be sincere and passionate.
4. Be considerate of the program.
5. Be funny.

My sister did an incredible job with my father. She provided so much love and care for him and I just want to say publicly to my sister, thank you for all that you did. You were a great daughter and I hope that I one day have a daughter who will be as loving to me as you were to Daddy.

I also want to acknowledge my mother. She did her absolute best for my father. There is no doubt about that. My father had it good, y'all. He really did, because my mother held him down. A few years ago there was a term of endearment in hip-hop for a woman who stuck by her man, no matter what. She was called a "ride-or-die chick." Well, to borrow a phrase from hip-hop culture (and I am sure my mother would never describe herself as such)—my mother was a "ride-or-die chick" in the most loving sense of the phrase.

I want to thank the doctors and nurses who provided care for my father at both Memorial Sloan-Kettering and at St. Catherine Hospital. I also want to thank the home nurses and hospice nurses that took care of him while he was at home where he wanted to be.

I want to thank everyone who came out to visit my father at the hospital and at home. Thank you for sending cards, flowers, fruit baskets, cookies, and for praying for him, for believing in him, and supporting him. It meant a lot to my father that so many people came to visit during his illness.

▶ [Jackie Hurt and Byron at Sundance]

I want to thank my wife Kenya for all her support over the past few years, and especially over the past few weeks. You really came through for us in the last couple weeks of my father's life. We could not have been so effective in helping take care of him without you. I appreciate you more than you know.

There are ten things I must say that I think define the legacy of my father:

1. He was extremely intelligent. He was a complex thinker.
2. He was a caring man. He loved his family, he loved his brothers, he loved his clients, he loved his community, and he loved Black people.
3. He carried himself with dignity all the way to the end.
4. He loved food and he loved to eat. In fact, he is probably hovering above us at an all-you-can-eat buffet right now, watching this entire service. I will miss going to Charlie Brown's for lunch, where we would go to eat together for some father/son time.
5. He had a great sense of humor.
6. He was a spiritually mature man.
7. He had an incredible, unbreakable will.
8. He was an extremely hard worker.
9. He was interested in social issues, and politics, and concerned about the world around him.
10. And he loved life.

I just can't say enough about my father. He was an extraordinary man. Anyone who knows my father knows that he was not your average person. I enjoyed listening to him because he was full of so much knowledge and history. Having my father was like hav-

"WHO

— WOULD I HAVE BEEN WITHOUT THIS —

MAN'S PRESENCE?"

ing Cornel West or Henry Louis Gates, Jr., or Michael Eric Dyson right at your fingertips. My father was an intellectual and he had a tremendous amount of intellectual hardware. He was a deep man. He had an incredible ability to place things and people into a larger context. He was not a simple-minded man, nor did he see things in black-and-white. If you asked my father a simple question, you would walk away with a very complex answer. He had the ability to see the nuances in life and in the world. He was exceptional on so many levels.

He worked with his hands. There were few things he could not fix with his own hands, and if he couldn't fix it himself, he knew somebody or knew where to go to fix it. He was a gifted painter and spackler. His hands were rough, so that my hands could be soft. As a teenager, I worked with him on many jobs and it was there where I learned so much about him and so much about life. He was a perfectionist. He got the job done right. He never painted a house for the customer; he painted a house for the next painter to see twenty or thirty years down the line. He taught me about goal setting. He would set me up in a room that needed to be painted and he would have me set a goal for how much time I would be in that room. He is the reason I am such a goal-oriented person.

He was an incredibly hard worker. He worked hard for many years so that he could provide for his wife and children, and that meant a lot to him.

I interviewed my father for my documentary *I Am a Man: Black Masculinity in America*, and in that interview he revealed that his greatest ambition in life was to be a father. That was such a powerful statement to me and it led me to ask this question: Who would I have been without this man's presence?

In fact, BECAUSE of my father's presence:

I am not a drug dealer

I am not a thief

I am not a liar

I am not without goals

I am not a wife beater

In jail

Hopeless

Aimless

Jobless

An alcoholic or a drug addict

A gossiper

An excuse maker

A derelict

Or lazy

And BECAUSE of the presence of my father:

I have sense of purpose

I have a mission in life

I am a goal setter

A civic leader

A creative being

A visionary

A hard worker

A humanitarian

An educator

A filmmaker

An activist

I have a purpose-driven life

I am an achiever

I have courage
I am a risk taker
I am committed to the pursuit of my dreams
I have a plan for myself and my family
I am going places in life because of the
presence of my father and my mother.

Thank God for my father. No, he was not a perfect man. He had his issues. He had trials and tribulations that he had to overcome, but he overcame them. He grew. He evolved. He was an overcomer. He overcame the obstacles that came his way. He was a great man of faith. He was spiritually mature.

We all learned so much from him. Even until his dying day he was teaching us how to fight, how to have faith, how to have courage, how to persevere; even as he battled cancer he taught us. He taught us how to deal with sickness, pain, and affliction. He taught us to be brave in the face of an unfortunate circumstance.

Even in death, right now, in this moment, he is teaching us all by our testimonies.

How many people in this church has this man inspired today? How many people in this church has this man prayed for? Prayed with? How many people in this church has my father influenced in a positive way? How many people in this church loved my father? How many people in this church had their homes painted by my father? Served on a committee with my father? Laughed with my father? Joked with my father? Cried with my father? How many people in this church did my father give advice to? How many people in this church confided in my father? How many people in this church did my father read scripture to? How many people in this room did my father challenge to think differently? If my father did any of those things for you, YOU SHOULD BE ON YOUR FEET to celebrate this man's life. He lived a great life; he married and stayed committed to his only wife. He loved, honored, and respected his children. He raised his children. He served his church. He served his community. He loved life and fought—even battled—to live until his very last breath. Give this man a standing ovation for living and welcome him into his new life, eternal life.

■

The Old Man

▶   JELANI COBB

The old man had huge hands.

They were hands that made a statement, all out of proportion with even his large body, looking like the good Lord had fashioned him from a Diego Rivera mural. Women, he would tell me devilishly, draw inferences from these kinds of hands. My father was born in 1919 in Hazlehurst, Georgia. His biography was inscribed in those hands—not in the hazy metaphysics of palm reading, but literally. The last digit of the left ring finger was permanently swollen, a lifelong reminder of a fastball that got away from him when he was a teenaged catcher. The knuckles were large, time-roughened orbs, a product of his years as a young heavyweight barnstorming through Florida during the Great Depression. There was a semicircular scar on the outside of one palm. He earned his living as an electrician and a spike he was using to break through a concrete wall jabbed through the flesh of his hand. Sixty years spent pulling cable and driving spikes will leave you with palms marked like stigmata.

He was nearly fifty years old when I was born, a generation

ear a watch: older than the fathers of the young men I went to school with. Early on, his age was the subject of adolescent taunts—until I learned to invert the insult: "Yeah, my father was forty-nine when I was born—you think your father will have anything left in the

A man tank when he hits that age?" There were times when I didn't want to be clever. Like the time when my eighth-grade nemesis Andre Brown called my father a cripple and my right hand ensured he regretted those words.

It might be because he was literally from a different era that I was one of the few black boys I knew in my South Queens, N.Y., neighborhood **must be** with a father in the household. The writer bell hooks has argued that black men of the generation born after World War II lost touch with the more gentle virtues that their fathers understood, replacing it with a type of boisterous masculinity that was, at its core, altogether more fragile. That might explain why the man who kept his boxer's physique well into his fifties, and who at age sixty-eight, tossed a crack fiend onto the pavement for menacing women in the neighborhood. He **responsible** was also secure enough to do the majority of the cooking and get his children ready for school each morning.

My earliest recollection in life is my small fingers engulfed by my

his time." father's hand as I learned to scrawl the alphabet. Knowledge—the formal kind that comes from places with manicured lawns and buildings with columns—held an almost mystical significance for those

generations of black people from which it had been withheld. My father was not educated by the standards of this society, but he was the best teacher I've ever met. His fear that he would pass on before I was grown made imparting wisdom to his youngest child the utmost priority. The sentences that began with some variation of "Boy, I might not be around to explain this to you years from now, so pay attention" are innumerable. If you want it distilled, these are the things he taught me:

▸ Never get into something until you've figured out how to get out of it.

▸ Wear a watch: A man must be responsible for his time.

▸ If that happens, try thinking about baseball.

▸ Cover it. No matter what she tells you.

▸ The Mets first and only; if absolutely necessary, the Yankees.

▸ The wrong woman can throw out more with a teaspoon than you can bring in with a wheelbarrow.

▸ A relationship is a compromise; if you always want it your way you also want to be alone.

▸ The fact that you know it don't mean you're supposed to say it.

▸ Trust everyone, but make sure you cut the cards.

▸ If it comes to blows, never, ever stop swinging.

But these are arid quotes. Understanding the meaning of fatherhood through collections of words is like thinking you understand a baseball game because you know how many pitches were thrown or the number of runs that were scored. The truth of the game lies

▸ [Distinguished gentlemen: Jelani and his father]

in what happens between pitches; the truth is the beauty of the pitcher's form, the arc of a curveball, and the internal rhythm of the game itself. What I took from my father was only partially verbal. The rest lay in the quiet reassurance that he was around, sitting on the front step with a beer, dispensing color commentary on the world as it passed by. Or the inferences I drew about the importance of work when I saw the old man, gray-haired and weary, but nonetheless heading out to pull cable in fourteen-degree weather.

In short, I learned the meaning of heroism.

We know, or ought to know by now, that heroes need not be perfect—just better than their circumstances would have them be. These were the circumstances: a man with three grades of book learning who had a family to feed and willingness to do hard work. He raised his first son, my brother Alan, by himself before he met and married my mother. He raised her two children, my brother Victor, and my sister Valerie as his own, never once making a distinction among us. The circumstance was a man whose eldest son returned from Vietnam hooked on heroin and died of AIDS in 1980. The old man sank into an abyss of despair and alcoholism that lasted three years. And for me, that era between 1980 and 1983 taught me that the term "flawed hero" is redundant. Two weeks after he quit drinking, a businessman hired my father to wire a liquor store. We needed the money, so he packed his tools and spent a four days in a basement filled with every variety of booze under the sun. He finished the job and walked out of that building certain that he was no longer a drinker. I walked away from that building certain that a man is not the one who has never fallen, but the one who has never failed to get up.

It is clear—as clear as gin—that we men of the hip-hop generation suffer from a hero deficit. We see this reality in hip-hop, where young men cling to the dead totems of failed manhood. We see it in our families and our spiraling out-of-wedlock birthrates. It is present in the lives of nearly one million incarcerated black men. Beneath our bombast and bravado lies a quiet truth: we are fragile and afraid and seek a way to become our own heroes.

My father passed on in 1992 when I was twenty-three years old. Toward the end, when he could barely speak, he motioned for the nurse to come near. We thought he needed more pain medication. He struggled to form his words. I had grown into an identical six-foot-three-inch frame. I carried his same outsized hands and I had fought and clawed my way into those buildings with the columns and manicured lawns. I could've told him that I knew times would not be easy, but that I would never, ever stop swinging. I could have told him that I would earn a PhD and take something that this world had refused my old man. He would explain that this was what he struggled for; the point beneath the stated and unspoken wisdom. Not simply a sheet of paper with Latin phrases inscribed, but a way of living in the world with unstooped shoulders. But he did not say this outright; instead he rasped to the nurse "My son . . . Howard University."

■

About the Contributors

▸ AARON LLOYD

Aaron Lloyd is a freelance writer, screenwriter, and filmmaker. He has written about hip-hop music artists for over a decade, including Left Eye of TLC and A Tribe Called Quest. His articles have appeared in *Rap Pages*, Vibe.com, and other outlets. Lloyd will write, produce, and release his debut film, a forty-five-minute short, in 2008. Aaron was a founding and executive board member of Black Nia F.O.R.C.E., a community and cultural organization, and was co-owner of the writing service company Scribble Scrabble Entertainment. Currently, Lloyd lives in Freeport, N.Y., with his wife, educator Michelle Lloyd.

▸ ADISA BANJOKO

Adisa Banjoko, author of *Lyrical Swords: Hip Hop and Politics in the Mix*, is a leading voice on issues of political, social, and religious trends in Hip-Hop. A respected journalist for more than fifteen years, his writing has appeared in *The Source, San Francisco Chronicle, XXL, Vibe, Yoga Journal, Pacific News Service, Onthemat.com,* and *Allhiphop.com.* Known as The Bishop of Hip Hop, Banjoko has lectured at countless universities, including Harvard, Stanford, Brown, and many others. He also lectures in prisons and juvenile hall facilities. In 2006, he founded the Hip-Hop Chess Federation, using music, chess, and martial arts to promote unity, strategy, and nonviolence. For more information, visit his Web site at **www.hiphopchessfederation.org**.

▸ ALFORD A. YOUNG, JR.
Alford A. Young, Jr., is Arthur F. Thurnau Professor and Associate Professor of Sociology in the Center for Afro-American and African Studies at the University of Michigan. He was born in 1966 and raised in New York City, where he attended Catholic elementary and secondary schools. He has published *The Minds of Marginalized Black Men: Making Sense of Mobility, Opportunity, and Future Life Chances* and is devoted to writing and teaching about the plight of Black men in American society. He is married to Carla O'Connor and is the father of Alford III (age 9) and Kai Alexander (age 4).

▸ BAKARI KITWANA
Bakari Kitwana is a journalist, activist, and political analyst. His essays have appeared in many publications, including *The Village Voice*, the *Los Angeles Times*, the *Boston Globe*, and *The Progressive*. He authored *The Hip-Hop Generation: Young Blacks and the Crisis in African American Culture* and most recently *Why White Kids Love Hip-Hop*. He's been the Editorial Director of Third

World Press, Executive Editor of *The Source*, and is cofounder of the first ever National Hip-Hop Political Convention (Newark, 2004). He holds a BA and two Master's degrees (English and teaching). He has appeared on CNN, PBS, and countless other outlets. For more information, visit **www.myspace.com/bakarikitwana**.

▸ BILL STEPHNEY

Bill Stephney created one of Hip Hop's first radio shows, *The Mr. Bill Show* (Adelphi University, 1982). Later he joined Def Jam Records, eventually becoming president (leading the careers of LL Cool J, Public Enemy, and others). Currently, he dedicates much of his time to acting as a family advocate. He has also served on the board of directors for the National Fatherhood Initiative. He has appeared as a commentator on every major television network and has been published by the *New York Times*, *Vibe*, and others. He lives in New Jersey with his wife, Tanya Cepeda, and their three children.

▸ BYRON HURT

Byron Hurt is an award-winning documentary filmmaker, published writer, and antisexist activist. His highly acclaimed film, *Hip-Hop: Beyond Beats and Rhymes* premiered at the Sundance Film Festival and was broadcast nationally on the PBS series *Independent Lens*. Hurt is also a longtime gender violence prevention educator and has been featured in the *New York Times*, *the Michael Baisden Show*, CNN, *ABC World News*, and countless community-based, regional, and national media outlets. Byron has lectured at more than one hundred colleges and trained thousands of people on gender, race, and violence issues. For more information, go to his Web site at **www.bhurt.com** or **www.myspace.com/beyondbeatsandrhymes**.

▸ CHEO TYEHIMBA

Cheo Tyehimba is an award-winning journalist, author, activist, and educator. He has written or reported for Time Inc. and *Entertainment Weekly*, and was a senior editor of *Code*. He's taught writing at the University of San Francisco and The City College of New York, where he earned an MA in Creative Writing. His writing has been published in the *Washington Post*, the *San Francisco Bay Guardian*, *People*, *Savoy*, *O—The Oprah Magazine*, *George*, *Vibe*, and *Essence*, among others. His short story collection, *When It Is*, will be published in spring 2008. He is a husband, father, and son. For more information, please visit **www.whatchusay.com** or **www.forwardevermedia.com**.

▸ DAVEY D.

Davey D is a historian, journalist, deejay, and activist. He's been down with Hip Hop since 1977. Currently he is the webmaster for one of the oldest and largest Hip Hop Internet sites, Davey D's Hip Hop Corner. Its writings are referenced and quoted all around the world. Davey is also program director of *Breakdown FM*, an internet radio show specializing in the examination of Hip-Hop and politics. Davey has been featured on BET Television, VH1 Television, BBC Radio, Fox News, CNN, ABC, and many others. He graduated from UC Berkeley and is currently working to bridge the digital divide. For more information, visit **www.daveyd.com** or **www.myspace.com/daveyd**.

▸ DION "SHOWTIME" CHAVIS

Media professional Dion "Showtime" Chavis has become the voice that listeners and readers have come to recognize as their own. Born and raised in Norfolk, Virginia, Showtime was the product of a single-parent home and raised by his mother. After losing his father at an early age, Showtime began to lean on the culture of Hip Hop as a way to fill the void that was left by his father's death. Showtime is an accomplished radio professional and blogger who uses his voice to help guide the lives of today's youth. For more information, visit **www.thatott.com** or **www.myspace.com/showtime757**.

▸ JAMES PETERSON

James Peterson, PhD, is an Assistant Professor of English at Bucknell University. Dr. Peterson, assisting Dr. Cornel West, delivered the "Hip Hop Studies" lectures at Princeton University and has guest-lectured with Dr. Michael Eric Dyson at the University of Pennsylvania. For his expertise, Dr. Peterson has been featured on/in BET, BET.com, *The Michael Eric Dyson Show*, *The Michael Baisden Show*, Fox News, MSNBC, ABC News, ESPN, the PBS documentary *Hip-Hop: Beyond Beats and Rhymes*, and many other outlets He has also been published, featured, or quoted in *Black Arts Quarterly*, *XXL*, *Vibe*, the *Wall Street Journal*, and various other publications.

▸ KEVIN POWELL

Kevin Powell is an activist, poet, essayist, public speaker, hiphop historian, and businessman. A product of extreme poverty, welfare, fatherlessness, and a single mother–led household, he is a native of Jersey City and was educated at New Jersey's Rutgers University. He is currently a student at Pace University, where he is finishing his BA in Liberal Studies. Kevin Powell is a longtime resident of Brooklyn, New York, and it is from his base in New York City that Powell has published eight books, including his most recent poetry collection, *No Sleep Till Brooklyn*. He can be reached at kevin@kevinpowell.net.

KEVIN WILLIAMS

Born in Warwick, New York, Kevin Williams received his BS degree in Accounting from Howard University. He was a founding member of the community and cultural organization, Black Nia F.O.R.C.E. Kevin also served as vice president of The Cultural Initiative Incorporated, the organizers of the first national conference on Hip-Hop (1991). For over a decade, Kevin has worked as an educator in the underserved Harlem community. He currently resides in the Bronx, New York, and is married to Shawn Bailey-Williams. He is the proud father of an energetic two-year-old son and a nineteen-year-old daughter who attends a historically Black college/university (HBCU).

LASANA OMAR HOTEP

Lasana Omar Hotep is a lecturer, consultant, and entrepreneur with a commitment to inciting critical thought about society, culture, and politics. His areas of expertise include Hip-hop history, Leadership Development, and African-American culture. He is the founder, principal owner, and lead consultant of Hotep Consultants. Lasana, along with Alonzo Jones, developed the nationally recognized recruitment and retention program, African American Men of Arizona State University (AAMASU). He currently serves as a Student Success Coordinator in the Multicultural Student Center at Arizona State University in Tempe, Arizona. He lives with his wife Dr. Renee V. Hotep in Mesa, Arizona. Contact Lasana at **www.lasanahotep.com** or **at www.myspace.com/lasana**.

LOREN HARRIS

Loren Harris is the Program Officer at the Ford Foundation, focusing on Adolescent Sexual and Reproductive Health. Harris has served as Associate Program Officer for the Mott Foundation.

There he designed and implemented the *Fathers at Work Initiative*, a $12 million national project. Harris holds a BA in U.S. History from Queens College and a Master's in Public Administration from Fairleigh Dickinson University. As philanthropist, he gives his time, talent, and treasure to various boards and local organizations. Loren is also a partner to his wife of fifteen years and a parent to four wonderful children.

▸ LUMUMBA AKINWOLE-BANDELE

Lumumba Akinwole-Bandele is a father, husband, DJ, concert producer, and community organizer from Brooklyn, now residing in Texas. Lumumba was a student at Brooklyn's premier Black independent school, Uhuru Sasa Shule. Bandele served as Director of Programs at the Franklin H. Williams Caribbean Cultural Center, is a member of the New Afrikan People's Organization, and of the Malcolm X Grassroots Movement. As a representative of MXGM, Lumumba cofounded Black August: A Celebration of Hip Hop and our Freedom Fighters Benefit Concert. Akinwole-Bandele has a degree in Black Studies from City College/CUNY and a Master's in Human Service from Lincoln University. For more information, visit **www.myspace.com/lumumbarevolution**.

▸ MO BEASLEY

Performance poet and educator Mo Beasley has over twenty years experience in sexuality, race, manhood, and arts advocacy work. He has lectured or facilitated workshops for countless institutions, ranging from SCO/Family Dynamics to Kaiser Permanente to New York University. He has been featured at the Blue Note, Minton's, Nuyorican Poets Café, Joe's Pub, and many other stages. Select media include NPR, BETJ, XM Radio, Hallmark Channel, Fox

News, rolling out, and others. In 2006, the *New York Daily News* selected Mo as one of "50 Unsung New York Heroes." He is also coauthor of the critically acclaimed play *No Good ~~Nigga~~ Bluez*. For more information, visit his official website at **www.mobeasley.com** or **www.myspace.com/mobeasleymusic**.

▸ RHYMEFEST

Rhymefest, one of the most intelligent and humorous rappers on the freestyle battle circuit, was born in Chicago. He dropped out of high school, then earned his GED and later enrolled in college. His girlfriend became pregnant, so they married and he worked low-paying jobs to support his family. Fest never abandoned his music. In 2005, he collaborated with longtime friend Kanye West on "Jesus Walks" (on West's *The College Dropout*). Rhymefest then earned a Grammy for Best Rap Song. Rhymefest's debut, *Blue Collar*, was released in 2006 to great acclaim. His second album, *El Che*, is due in 2008. For more information, please visit **www.rhymefest.com**.

▸ SADDI KHALI

Saddi Khali is a writer/performer/photographer/activist from New Orleans. He has been published in *Dark Eros* and *Obsidian II*, among others, and has been a featured performer on HBO's *Def Poetry Jam*, and the historic Apollo Theater's Salon Series. He is currently touring with "Uprooted: The Katrina Project," and heading an organization that creates and promotes healthy images of people of color in the media. For more information, visit **www.myspace.com/saddikhali**.

▸ SHAUN NEBLETT

Shaun Neblett, based in Harlem of Panamian parents, is a playwright, youth theater coordinator, and Founder/Artistic Director of Our Id Theater. He has shared the platform with Woodie King, Jr., Amiri Baraka, and Ed Bullins and his work has been produced by P.S. 122, Provincetown Playhouse, the National Black Theater, House of Tribes Theater, and other regional theaters. His play *This is About a Boy's Fears* was produced at the Young Playwrights Festival at the Joseph Papp Public Theater. Currently, Shaun is working on seven plays in tribute to the classic albums of seven hip-hop artists.

▸ STEVEN G. FULLWOOD

Steven G. Fullwood has been an archivist at the Schomburg Center for Research in Black Culture in New York since 1998. He is the founder of the Black Gay and Lesbian Archive and project director of the Hip-Hop Archive Project. Fullwood is the author of *FUNNY* (2004), coeditor of *Think Again* (2003), and the founder and publisher at Vintage Entity Press. For over a decade, his writing has appeared in *Library Journal, Black Issues Book Review, XXL, Vibe, and Lambda Book Report*. In 2005 Fullwood was honored with a *New York Times* Librarian Award. For more information, visit **www.stevengfullwood.org** or **www.vepress.com**.

▸ TALIB KWELI

In the '90s he was half of the rap duo Black Star (with Mos Def). Today, Talib Kweli (from Brooklyn) stills makes music that educates and entertains simultaneously. Both Jay-Z and 50 Cent named Kweli as one of their favorite rappers. *Ear Drum*, his sixth album (and the first released on his own label) is a career-defining work. Kweli has two gold albums with the majority of his topics focusing on "black self-love, black self-esteem, and black self worth." After establishing himself as a visionary, Kweli and manager Corey Smyth created and launched the record label Blacksmith Music. For more information, visit the official Web site, **www.talibkweli.com**.

▸ THABITI BOONE

Thabiti Boone is an author, activist, humanitarian, former basketball star, and minister. He defied the odds of taking his daughter to college, as a teenage single father, balancing fatherhood, education, student leadership, and basketball stardom, including sacrificing his NBA dreams to raise her. He is a passionate national speaker and voice on fatherhood, Black men, and world issues. He founded a charitable foundation that impacts young people. Some of his accolades include 2007 National Martin Luther King, Jr. Man of the Year and 2007 CNN Global Hero. He has been the subject of books, publications, documentaries, TV, and print media. For more information, visit **www.thabitienterprises.com**.

▸ TIMOTHY D. JONES

Timothy D. encompasses the essence of hip-hop as a creator of various educational initiatives that use aspects of hip-hop culture. "Educate, Evaluate, and Elevate" is the approach that Timothy takes to work whether it is running a Teen Program at Martha's Table in Washington, D.C.; serving as Director of Community Outreach and Social Entrepreneurship for the ELI Institute (Howard University); or being an Ordained Minister at The Believers Worship Center in Forestville, Maryland. A family that loves him, a world that needs him, and his Lord that saved him is the "Beat of Life"—Jones' consulting company. For more information, visit, **www.myspace.com/timothydjones**.

▶ WILLIAM JELANI COBB

William Jelani Cobb, PhD is an Associate Professor of History at Spelman College. He specializes in post–Civil War African American history, twentieth-century American politics, and the history of the Cold War. A highly respected and widely published essayist, Cobb is also the author of *To The Break of Dawn: A Freestyle on the Hip Hop Aesthetic*, as well as *The Devil & Dave Chappelle and Other Essays*. He is editor of *The Essential Harold Cruse: A Reader*, which was listed as a 2002 *Notable Book of The Year by Black Issues Book Review*. He resides in Atlanta, Georgia. For more information, visit his official Web site at **www.jelanicobb.com** or **www.myspace.com/jelanicobb**.

Books for
Further Reading

▸ *Becoming Dad: Black Men and the Journey to Fatherhood*
BY LEONARD PITTS

▸ *Between Father and Son: An African American Fable*
BY ERIC V. COPAGE

▸ *Black Fatherhood II: Black Women Talk about Their Men*
BY EARL OFARI HUTCHINSON, JOHNATHAN SMITH (ILLUSTRATOR)

▸ *Black Fatherhood: Reconnecting with Our Legacy*
BY DANA E. ROSS

▸ *Black Fatherhood: The Guide to Male Parenting*
BY EARL OFARI HUTCHINSON, ALBERT FENNELL (ILLUSTRATOR)

▸ *Black Fathers in Contemporary American Society:
Strengths, Weaknesses, and Strategies for Change*
BY OBIE CLAYTON (EDITOR), RONALD B. MINCY (EDITOR),
DAVID BLANKENHORN (EDITOR)

▸ *Black Fathers: A Call for Healing*
BY KRISTIN CLARK TAYLOR

▸ *Black Fathers: An Invisible Presence in America*
BY MICHAEL E. CONNOR AND JOSEPH WHITE (EDITORS)

▸ *Black Men, Obsolete, Single, Dangerous?:*
The Afrikan American Family in Transition
BY HAKI R. MADHUBUTI

▸ *Commitment: Fatherhood in Black America*
BY CAROLE PATTERSON, ARVARH E. STRICKLAND, CLYDE RUFFIN,
MINION K. C. MORRISON, ANTHONY BARBOZA, MARLENE PERCHINSKE

▸ *Conversations with John Edgar Wideman*
BY JOHN EDGAR WIDEMAN, BONNIE TUSMITH (EDITOR)

▸ *Critical Memory: Public Spheres, African American Writing,*
and Black Fathers and Sons in America
BY HOUSTON A. BAKER

▸ *Daddy Goes to Work*
BY JABARI ASIM (AUTHOR); AARON BOYD (ILLUSTRATOR)

▸ *Daddy, We Need You Now!: A Primer on African-American*
Male Socialization
BY HERMAN A. SANDERS

▸ *Daughters of Men: Portraits of African-American Women and Their Fathers*
BY RACHEL VASSEL

- *I Got Your Back: A Father and Son Keep it Real About Love, Fatherhood, Family, and Friendship*
  BY EDDIE LEVERT, SR., GERALD LEVERT, LYAH LEFLORE

- *In Daddy's Arms I Am Tall: African Americans Celebrating Fathers*
  BY JAVAKA STEPTOE (ILLUSTRATOR)

- Losing Absalom
  BY ALEXS D. PATE

- *My Soul to His Spirit: Soulful Expressions from Black Daughters to Their Fathers*
  BY MELDA BEATY (EDITOR)

- *New Black Man: Rethinking Black Masculinity*
  BY MARK ANTHONY NEAL

- *Pop: A Celebration of Black Fatherhood*
  BY CAROL ROSS

- *Real Dads Stand Up! What Every Single Father Should Know About Child Support, Rights and Custody*
  BY ALICIA M. CROWE

- *Sacred Bond: Black Men and Their Mothers*
  BY KEITH MICHAEL BROWN

- *Song for My Father: Memoir of an All-American Family*
  BY STEPHANIE STOKES OLIVER

BE A FATHER TO YOUR CHILD

Edited by April R. Silver

Book design by Timothy Goodman

Soft Skull Press

2008